The Compassion of the Christ

SP

Bible versions used

The author has used mainly the **NRSV** (New Revised Standard Version) and the **NKJV** (New King James Version), but a number of quotations represent free translations from the Greek by the author.

Copyright © 2004
First published 2004

All rights reserved. No part of this publication
may be reproduced in any form without prior
permission from the publisher.
British Library Cataloguing in Publication Data.
A catalogue record for this book is available
from the British Library.

ISBN 1-904685-05-6

Published by
The Stanborough Press Limited,
Alma Park, Grantham, Lincs.

Printed in Thailand

The Compassion of the Christ

by
Keith Burton

About the author:

Keith Augustus Burton PhD is associate pastor at the Madison Mission church and a member of the General Conference Biblical Research Institute Committee. He is married and has two children. He has preached and lectured in Europe, North America, Africa and the Caribbean, and has written over a hundred articles and several books. For the past ten years Dr Burton has taught classes on the life and ministry of Jesus at Oakwood College, Huntsville, Alabama.

Contents

Introduction — 6

The Spirit of the Lord is upon me — 9

For God so loved the world — 24

Neither do I condemn you — 44

Do you want to be healed? — 66

Blessed are the persecuted — 85

We have an Advocate — 105

Conclusion — 122

Introduction

'When he saw the crowds, he had compassion for them, because they were harassed and helpless, like sheep without a shepherd. Then he said to his disciples, "The harvest is plentiful, but the labourers are few; therefore ask the Lord of the harvest to send out labourers into his harvest." '
Matthew 9:36-38, NRSV

Mel Gibson's *The Passion of the Christ* has already gone down in history as one of the most successful films ever produced. The film industry has not seen the public respond so favourably to an overtly religious film since the 1950s with the release of Cecil B. DeMille's, *The Ten Commandments* and William Wyler's *Ben Hur*. While attracting a lot of negative criticism, Martin Scorsese's 1988 sacrilegious depiction of the final thoughts of Jesus in *The Last Temptation of Christ* was totally incapable of garnering the massive following of *The Passion of the Christ*.

In this surprise blockbuster, Gibson devotes most of the movie to the portrayal of the final twenty-four hours in the life of Christ. Starting with the agonising prayer of Jesus in the Garden of Gethsemane and an encounter with an androgynous Satan, the movie transitions to repeated scenes of unspeakable violence that were able simultaneously to evoke both sympathy and disgust from the most hardened viewers. One viewer in the American mid-west was apparently so disturbed by the graphic scenes that she suffered a fatal heart attack in the cinema. Echoing the sentiment of Luke in the preface to his gospel, Gibson claims that his aim was to present an accurate picture of Christ's suffering. In his effort to maintain authenticity, the entire script was in Latin and Aramaic, interpreted to the viewers via subtitles.

Gibson is probably pleased to hear the accolades of those who extol the movie as the closest thing to a visual Bible. However, the reviews are not as dazzling from professional theologians, who are quick to expose Gibson's failure to produce a precise portrayal of first-century Palestine and the events surrounding the crucifixion. Among other things, Gibson has been chastised for replacing Greek with Latin as the *linguae franca* in first-century Palestine and overstating the amount of suffering that a human being could possibly endure.

While I am pleased that the movie has awakened attention to the life of Christ and the Christian message, I am concerned that people may leave with the impression that the suffering of Christ is all that mattered in his life. This was just one day in the life of a thirty-four-year-old man who had just completed three-and-a-half years of public ministry. If all that matters is his suffering, then any number of people who have been viciously abused to a greater extent than our Saviour could qualify as vehicles for atonement. Contemplating his twelve hours of suffering is important, but it must not eclipse the significance of his very meaningful life. This book proposes that we can only appreciate his suffering if we understand his purpose for living.

As we investigate the life and teachings of Christ, we quickly learn that Jesus' long path to his passion was occupied by acts of *com*passion. In fact, it is impossible to understand his *passion* without comprehending the extent of his *compassion* – a compassion that led him to relinquish his kingly, universal throne and divine status, and identify with a race of sinners who were in desperate need of God's grace. A compassion that he hoped would spread like a benign epidemic to those who would become his disciples throughout the annals of history. Indeed, it is for these that this book has been written – people who profess to be a part of the loving body of Christ.

All who read the book are encouraged to move from passive reflection on the life of Jesus to active participation in his ministry. Each chapter carefully aims to transmit the major teachings of Jesus on several subjects, and shares ways in which theory can be transformed into practice. Starting with a call to compassionate concern for the world's downtrodden, the book moves to discussions on relating to people of other faiths; relationships with sinners within and outside the church; the significance of healing in the propagation of the Gospel; the harassing obstacles that challenge faithful Christians; and the continued demonstration of compassion by a Christ who intercedes for his siblings.

Every chapter ends with a few reflection questions and practical suggestions about how the principles discussed in the chapter can be applied to everyday life.

While none of us can participate in Jesus' passion, it is hoped that all who encounter this book will be moved to share in his compassion as they make conscious decisions to live the gospel of Christ.

Chapter 1
The Spirit of the Lord is upon me

*'The Spirit of the Lord is upon me, because
he has anointed me to evangelise the poor,
he has sent me to proclaim emancipation to the
prisoners and restoration of sight to the blind,
he has commissioned me to emancipate the oppressed,
to proclaim the acceptable year of the Lord.'*
Luke 4:16-19.

I often find myself wondering if Jesus would have joined the March on Washington DC if he had been on earth in August 1963. I wonder if he would have been among those in Sharpville, South Africa, in that same year when the security forces mercilessly murdered innocent women and children who peacefully protested the unjust pass system that was enforced on them by a racist authority. I wonder if he would have sympathised with the early proponents of women's rights who campaigned for the right to vote, and the right to be compensated with equal pay for equal work. I wonder if he would have joined the pro-life lines outside the abortion clinics appealing for the right of unborn children to experience life. I wonder if he would have been instrumental in starting a soup kitchen, tutoring programme, and homeless shelter in his home church.

Many Christians look at these issues of social justice and

feel that, since the world is soon to end with the second coming, there is no need to get involved with the social ailments of society. They seem to have the peculiar idea that Jesus would rather we saturate the communities with doctrinal literature than join in efforts to better the lives of those in the community who are underprivileged. However, Jesus' life seems to counteract any notion that a person can be interested in the spiritual salvation of an individual and neglect the social reality of the individual's existence. The gospels portray a Jesus who was concerned with developing a just society.

Precedent for a just society had been given by God to the Israelites. The law of Moses is replete with laws that promoted a just society. God is concerned with justice, especially when it comes to empowering those who have nothing. He realised that some people will get carried away with their credit cards and live from paycheque to paycheque without being able to pay their necessary bills, and so he instituted a bankruptcy system whereby every seven years a creditor could cancel a person's debt. That person was given a chance to start again.

God also provided for the impoverished in the community, the widow and the orphan. As we see with the story of Ruth and Boaz, one of the societal laws of social justice stipulated that everything that the harvesters did not reap on the first run had to be given to the poor. The society that God envisioned was built on justice and equality and even the slaves had rights. If a master physically mutilated a slave, that slave would automatically be set free.

So concerned was God for the equal rights of all humans that he even demanded that the non-Israelite slave rest on the Sabbath along with everyone else in the house. As Charles Bradford has recognised in his book *Sabbath Roots: The African Connection*, God's prescription for the treatment of the slave proved that no human has the right to lord it over another. Symbolic of the new age, on the Sabbath the slave was just as important and unimportant as his master.

By the time of the New Testament, Palestine had been continuously raped and pillaged by foreign invaders. Furthermore, those in power were corrupt and only concerned with bettering their own financial condition. These realities meant that there was not much evidence of justice in this semi-autonomous society. The world in which Jesus was a part was characterised by inequity and oppression. Suffering and deprivation were the order of the day. It is estimated that approximately two-thirds of the population of the Roman Empire were either slaves or former slaves. The only person in imperial Rome who could experience real freedom was the citizen. Unless you were a citizen, you had no real rights. Any soldier could stop you on the street and demand that you carry his heavy luggage for a mile. Your daughters could be raped and there was nothing you could do about it.

Not only was social injustice a part of the political order, it was also expressed within the very communities of the Jews. Sick people were viewed as unclean and were not allowed within certain boundaries of the city. Women were second class citizens and had few established rights. In many ways they were like property. There was vast inequity between the wealthy Sadducees and the impoverished commoners. And even the religious structure was more concerned with making money than ministering to the sick and needy souls.

When Jesus preached his homecoming sermon in Nazareth, he chose as his text Isaiah 61:1-2: ' "The Spirit of the Lord is upon me, because he has anointed me to bring good news to the poor. He has sent me to proclaim release to the captives and recovery of sight to the blind, to let the oppressed go free, to proclaim the year of the Lord's favour."' A close analysis of this text demonstrates that each clause addresses a pertinent issue of social justice. In no uncertain terms, Jesus declared war against injustice in society.

Good News to the Poor

According to the text, Jesus' first mission was to bring *good news to the poor*. The very presence of poor people indicates social injustice. God did not create a world that was to mould itself after the capitalist ideal of the haves and the have-nots. He did not create a race where some would feel comfortable owning fleets of expensive cars and multi-million-dollar mansions, while other decent, hard working people would have no roof over their heads because they could not find work to pay the rent. God's society was one based on equality – socialist if you please. There was no place in God's society for poor people. However, as a result of sin, the seed of greed has been planted in the heart of many who feel that just because they donate a small portion of their income to charity (which may seem large to us), they have done enough.

Matthew 19:16-30 tells the story of the successful young politician. As far as his spiritual life was concerned, he was super righteous. He had kept all the commandments from his youth. He hadn't left the church like many of his friends. He double-tithed and was a strong financial supporter of the church programme. He was even responsible for the weekly Bible study groups at the local Rotary Club and Chamber of Commerce. This was the type of person who brought prestige to a church.

Jesus looked at the achievements on his impressive resumé and found there was one pertinent section missing.

That young man had no real experience for the occupation of the kingdom. He had no concern for the poor. As far as he was concerned, if they worked as hard as he, they could also be financially comfortable. They needed to stand on their own two feet and stop relying on the crutch of welfare. Why, if he were to give them handouts they would never be able to appreciate the decency of hard work! To distribute his wealth among them would have made him one of them, and he was not ready for that. He was prepared to sympathise with them and put a few banknotes in the offering plate for missions and the poor fund, but he was not willing to commit himself to the extent that would make him one of them.

As the young man's shadow slowly vanished in the rugged horizon, Jesus uttered a strange statement: ' "It is easier for a camel to go through the eye of a needle than for a rich man to enter the kingdom of God." ' (Matt 19:24.) Let's understand that Jesus did not make a general indictment against riches with this statement. He simply uttered a harsh reality. Many people who have numerous possessions find their fulfilment in the things of this earth. Selfishness compels them to splurge on expensive cars and precious stones that they hoard in their garages and safes in Beverly Hills, while their neighbours in the ghettoes struggle to find two pennies to rub together.

I am not suggesting that poverty is an indicator of a just society. Neither am I proposing that true justice is demonstrated in monastic asceticism. But I do feel that a just society is characterised by unselfishness. A society in which responsibility to the other is a part of each individual's psyche. I believe that the community described in Acts 2 is a reflection of this type of society. The believers understood the social imperatives of the Gospel and determined among themselves to ensure that the least among them was afforded the basics associated with life, liberty, and happiness. The poor among them were able to experience the gospel of the kingdom. They were able to enjoy some of the necessities that had been previously barred from them. The good news was that they did not have to remain in the 'caste of class', but could enjoy fulness of personhood with those from the other side of the tracks. Is there a lesson for us in this?

Emancipation to the Prisoners

The second tenet of Jesus' text involves the proclamation of *emancipation to those in prison*. This tenet should be understood in the context of Roman occupation, when a foreign power had established the rules in his house. Jesus, and the Jews of first-century Palestine were in many ways like the Native Americans whose country was invaded by a foreign enemy that established a government therein, and gave them the false feeling of independence as they restricted them to territorial homelands known as reservations. But in reality, these territorial homelands were like prisons without bars. While the people could socialise, work, and engage in political assembly, they were not free because they were under the iron fist of Rome.

Any society in which the indigenous population is controlled by a foreign power is unjust. The colonisation of America which subjugated the status of the Native Americans was unjust. Hitler's quest to control Europe by annexing all the nations that surrounded Germany was unjust. The occupation and colonisation of Africa by the English, Germans, and French was unjust. I believe that Jesus rejoiced when Europe was liberated from the dreaded threat of Hitler's *Dritte Reich*. I also believe that he rejoiced when Nelson Mandela was voted President of South Africa. He rejoiced because these victories indicated the commencement of the erosion of oppression.

Indeed, the very fact that Jesus was the Messiah was to signal the liberation of the political prisoners. When Peter uttered his declaration in Caesarea Philippi, professing that Jesus was 'the Messiah, the Son of the living God', he had dreams of a reversal of the political order. According to the prophecies of the Old Testament, and the rich legacy in non-biblical Jewish literature, the Messiah would ensure that Israel would be the head and not the tail. Peter anticipated the imminency of a kingdom in which he would be the jailer, and his former oppressors the prisoners. An era in which the kingdoms of Parthia, Ethiopia, Armenia, Venda, and Rome, would be vassals to the new, improved, and immortal Kingdom of Israel.

However, the Messiah did not make a political statement with his announcement of mass-clemency. His vision was not territorial, but universal. He knew that even the jailers were in prison. As Dr Martin Luther King realised, none can be free unless all are free. The very presence of prisons indicates terror and instability. They are a reminder of the sinful condition of humanity.

Messiah knew that the absence of prison bars did not mean freedom. The truth is that the bars that restrict are spiritual and surround the entire world. Paul recognises this when he writes that 'all of creation groans together for deliverance' (Rom. 8:22). The entire creation is in need of deliverance. Throughout his ministry, Jesus demonstrated that true liberation involves freedom from non-political forms of imprisonment. Many people choose to remain in prison even after they have been pardoned. They refuse to break loose from the chains that restrict and enjoy the fulness of life that can only be attained in Jesus Christ. No, true liberation is not merely a release from physical structures. It is not a pardon from the governor or the satisfaction of a sentence. True liberation is only realised through the One who is able to remove permanently the barriers that keep God's earthly creation in an incarcerated state.

If the political prisoner's heart has not been baptised in the blood of Jesus, more Nazis will arise. If the societal prisoner has not been rejuvenated by the empowering Spirit, she will become a repeat offender. But Jesus has come to release his creation from the prison house of sin and death. According to the apostle Peter, by Jesus' death he preached to those imprisoned spirits and announced their imminent pardon. We are further informed that at his resurrection he snatched the keys for the jail of Sheol from the hands of the master jailer, Satan. And Matthew lets us know that the first few parolees visited Jerusalem as a witness to Jesus' claim that he has the ability to 'release those in prison'.

While we celebrate with Noble Alexander, Nelson Mandela, Angela Davis, and the many other political prisoners who have experienced freedom; and while we pray for the host of others who have been unjustly incarcerated in Cuba, Angola, Yugoslavia, Russia, China, Nigeria, America, and countless other nations, let's not forget that the chains that really imprison are the chains of sin. We are only free when we ask the question with Paul, 'Who can release me from this body of death?' and are able to answer, 'Thanks be to God, who does it through his Son, Jesus Messiah!' (Rom. 7:25).

Recovery of Sight to the Blind
Another platform on which Jesus built his ministry involved the *recovery of sight to the blind*. This suggests a healing ministry. From the accounts of blind people we read about in the gospels, it seems as if many people who had lost

their sight were left to fend for themselves. This is also true for those who were afflicted with leprosy and other social ailments. They were ostracised and ignored by society. However, Jesus recognised that a society that ignores its sick and impaired is an unjust society. And so his ministry was characterised by caring and healing as he went from village to village with his mobile miracle clinic. He did not understand why there would be so much resistance to universal health care by a group of men on the hill — all of whom had 100% health coverage.

John tells us of the paralysed man Jesus met at the pool at Bethsaida. Along with many other sick people, this man was waiting for the pool to be disturbed by an angel so that he could jump in and receive healing. But he was alone. Although there were hundreds and thousands of healthy people living in Palestine, many of whom were probably members of his church, not one would take the time to stand vigil with him and assist him when the water moved.

The prevalent attitude towards sickness by first century Jews is further demonstrated in John's account of the man born blind (John 9:1-12). Upon passing this man, the disciples asked Jesus whose sin was responsible for his condition — the man's or his parents? Implicit in this inquiry is the assumption that every sickness is the result of personal sin. It is true that some sinful lifestyles do result in sickness and disease. There are consequences to certain choices.

However, the disciples' inquiry did not consider consequential illness. Theirs was not a question that saw a link between HIV and homosexuality or promiscuity. They were not associating arteriosclerosis or hypertension with tobacco, alcohol, and the consumption of animals. They had a shammaistic understanding of the relationship between sin and sickness. They thought that a child of an illicit affair would be physiologically affected. They thought that one who violated the Sabbath would suffer anatomical damage.

The logical opposite inference to the disciples' question is that wellness is an indication of personal righteousness. Jesus was to shatter this myth with his response, as he let them know that neither the man nor his parents were responsible for the sickness. The disciples quickly learnt that unrighteousness was not necessarily the root of sickness. In fact, when Jesus addressed the Scribes and Pharisees in Matthew 23, he let them know that the self-righteousness that drove them to call the infirmed 'unclean' was a sorry facade for their true sepulchered personalities.

Having said all this, I have to admit that the disciples were right in associating sickness with sin. However, it is not individual sin, but universal evil that is at the root of Downs Syndrome, Cancer, Strokes, Sickle Cell Disease, Multiple Sclerosis, AIDS, and the countless other ailments that threaten society. Sickness has its inception in the fall of humanity, and is one of many indicators that the sadistic Satan has temporary access into the affairs of humanity.

Before restoring sight to the man who had never been able to see, Jesus informed his disciples that the miracle would serve as a manifestation of the 'works of God'. Satan's sicknesses become extinct when confronted by God's glory. With his miracles of healing, Jesus demonstrated the atmosphere of the kingdom. Only a select few had the opportunity of being the healthy prototypes of the citizens who will inhabit the eschatological kingdom, but the prophet John lets us know that in the New Jerusalem there will be no sickness, dying or pain. No need for aspirins or antacids. No need for managed health care organisations. No need for insurance or co-payments.

But what do we do until then? How does Jesus' declaration of 'the recovery of sight to the blind' affect our Christian walk? I propose that we live out the vision of Jesus. In another chapter we will address the question of 'faith healing', but sharing the vision of Jesus does not only involve the supernatural; it demands interaction in the social sphere. It calls for those who claim to be the people of God to follow in the footsteps of Jesus as we dare to touch those whom others have called unclean. It affirms the ministries of ADRA, Mother Teresa's Sisters of Mercy, and others who sacrifice self for another's health. It beckons us to the bedside of the one afflicted with cancer, leprosy, or AIDS. It urges us to occupy our time in works of mercy, until Jesus comes to establish his sanitised and wholesome kingdom.

Freedom for the Oppressed

The fourth mandate in Jesus' declaration concerned *liberation for people who have been oppressed*. As mentioned earlier, the society of the Roman world was built on slavery. In fact, no capitalist society can exist without the practice of slavery and exploitation. Many of us enjoy the luxuries of western society, and people from all over the developing world yearn to move to western nations and walk the golden streets and taste the milk and honey that they see on the silver screen. However, what we do not realise is that most of the luxuries we enjoy are made possible by exploitation. Many industrialised nations were made great by the blood and sweat of slaves and exploited people. And you could not afford those fancy electronic gadgets and suave clothes if there was not someone in Taiwan, Indonesia, China, Mexico, Guatemala, or India, who did not have to work for a pittance in order to feed their families.

Jesus saw the slavery system and he declared it unjust. Those who claim that the Bible supports the institution of slavery are wrong. It is true that the various Bible authors uncritically described situations where slavery was practised. But do the stories of the slaves owned by the patriarchs and kings of Israel provide a justification for slavery? It is also true that the societal laws of the Pentateuch convey instructions concerning slaves. But do these indicate a blanket endorsement of slavery?

The pivotal point in the saga of Israel is the Exodus from Egypt where they had been the victims of oppressive exploitation. The God who created all people in His image identified with the oppressed and demanded that their oppressors liberate them. Divine inspiration testifies that the same God who liberated Israel also intervened on behalf of the millions of Africans who had been forcefully removed from their homeland and dispersed in hostile lands. I dare say that God also saw to it that the Ashkenazi Jews were saved from their oppressors during World War II.

As God, Jesus could not have endorsed any form of political slavery. The enslavement of another person gives the false notion that some people are superior to others. However, Jesus knew that God did not create a society that was built on class structures, but one that was classless. One in which people had mutual respect for one another.

In his eschatological vision of the household of God, the apostle Paul declares 'There is neither Jew nor Greek, there is neither slave nor free, there is neither male nor female; for you are all one in Christ' (Gal 3:28). In God's ideal society, social distinctions are abolished as people are seen as people. But until we get there, what should we do? In this world where social differences are so pronounced, and we use pejoratives like 'undeveloped' and 'third world' to describe the ones who enable our luxuries, how should we act?

Conclusion:
Proclamation of the Acceptable Year of the Lord

The final tenet of Jesus' ministry involves the announcement of the kingdom of God. In a sense, this tenet summarises the intent of the previous four. When the first four tenets are realised, the kingdom will be actualised. However, as we will see in a future chapter, this will not be our doing but God's. In spite of what the proponents of New Age philosophies are teaching, the society that is built on justice will have to originate and be maintained by one who is just. And as much as our egos may be bruised by my honesty, we have to admit that none of us is fit to be a part of a just society. As long as the tentacles of evil embrace this age, we can never experience equity, wholeness, and liberty.

However, this is not to say that we are not to live out proleptically the ideals of the eschatological kingdom. Indeed, the prophecy of the Great Judgement in Matthew 25:31-46 lets us know the seriousness of the call to social justice. In our confrontation of societal evil and unconditional acceptance of those who have been marginalised, we do the work of the kingdom. We become the hands and feet of our king.

While Jesus encourages us to practise justice and to be proactive in issues that impact the liberties of our fellow human beings, he realises that since Satan is still the temporary ruler of this world, no amount of effort on our part can ultimately and permanently transform societies. We wrestle not against flesh and blood; against political structures; against gang-bangers and crack houses; against rapists and racists; we wrestle against principalities and powers and spiritual wickedness in high places. He knows that the world's cities will not be ultimately transformed to communities of peace by human effort.

The compassionate Christ desires, rather, that those who claim to be members of the kingdom of God — the Church — should model the ideal society for all the world to see. He says, 'By this shall all people know that you are my disciples, if you have love, one for another'. A loving community is not going to discriminate on the basis of sex, ethnicity, age, or education. A loving community is not going to keep its door closed to a suffering world looking for refuge and shelter from the atrocities of society. A loving community will say with Christ, 'The Spirit of the Lord is upon us, for he has anointed us to preach good news to the poor. He has sent us to proclaim release to the captives and recovering of sight to the blind, to set at liberty those who are oppressed, to proclaim the acceptable year of the Lord.'

Reflect

1. If Jesus is coming again to establish God's eternal kingdom, why should Christians be concerned about the social ills in the world?
2. Should Christians involve themselves in pacifist protests and rallies against injustice in society?
3. Look at the labels on the clothes and appliances in your home and make a list of the countries in which they were made. How does this relate to a discussion on justice in society?
4. Some Christians feel it is their duty to renounce riches and share everything with the less fortunate. Is there anything inherently wrong with wealth?

Apply

1. Locate a local hospice or retirement home and commit to volunteering an hour each month to providing company for a lonely person.
2. Ask family members not to buy you gifts for a birthday or Christmas, but to send the money they would have spent to a charity of your choice.
3. Encourage your church to get involved in relevant ministries that address the needs of your immediate community.
4. Arrange a group in your church to send care packages to prisoners and their families on their birthdays and Christmas.

Chapter 2
For God so loved the world

*'"For God so loved the world
that he gave his only born Son,
so that whoever believes in him
should not perish but have eternal life.
For God did not send his Son into the world
to condemn the world, but to save it."'*
John 3:16-17.

The release of *The Passion of the Christ* has evoked charges of antisemitism from both Jewish and Christian leaders. For many, the memory of the Nazi holocaust remains a haunting warning of what can happen when a religious group is targeted as the scapegoat for societal ills. While the persecution of the Ashkenazi Jews and other religious minorities under Hitler's government must never be forgotten, it is also important to recognise that the persecution of Christ and his followers by the Jewish and Roman authorities is likewise historical reality. Nonetheless, it must also be remembered that those who presided over or partcipated in Christ's trial and crucifixion were merely acting as agents for every human being born from the creation of Adam to our present age. The clear message of salvation starts with the reality that '*all* have sinned and are coming short of the glory of God' (Rom. 3:23). We are *all* responsible for the death of Christ. As such, we are all indicted and stand in desperate need of the grace and forgiveness of God. Indeed, it is because of this very reality that the Bible declares that 'God loved *the world* so much, that he gave his only born Son, that whoever believes in him shall not perish but have eternal life' (John 3:16).

Those who claim to be believers in God's Son have a responsibility to share this good news with all of humanity. Unfortunately, an assessment of Christian history shows that this has not always been the case. Many who have interacted with Christians will never know that they are supposed to represent a God who really loves the entire world. Over the ages, Christians have not been the most tolerant people. As early as the second century when Christians sought independence from their Jewish identity, Christian writers wrote many negative things about Jews. In the following centuries they continued to express their distaste to the extent that certain segments of the church even gave up Sabbath observance and forsook dietary restrictions in order to distance themselves from their Jewish parentage.

Christian intolerance has also manifested itself in the Crusades of the Middle Ages where hundreds of thousands of Muslims were killed in the name of 'Jesus'. And it was also professed Christians who supported the transport of tens of millions of slaves to the Americas under the guise of saving the 'heathens.' The level of intolerance is even manifested in the intra-religious infighting that has Catholics and Protestants killing each other in Northern Ireland; Eastern Orthodox churches persecuting Evangelicals in Russia and Greece; and Evangelicals in North America claiming final authority over all Christians. The inability of some Christians to picture a God who loves all is also evidenced in the preaching of fundamentalist evangelists who restrict salvation to the enlightened few who belong to a particular Christian denomination.

Christian intolerance towards other religions is in no way justified by the ministry and teachings of Jesus. Although Jesus was born into a people who had been chosen by God, he was fully aware that the selection of Israel was for the purpose of being a blessing to the nations and not a hoarder of God's gifts. He did not come as a barrier to God's mercies, but as the doorway to salvation. The Bible is very clear that 'God did not send his Son into the world to condemn the world, but that the world through him might be saved' (John 3:17). As we saw in the previous chapter, God is not only concerned about the welfare of those who align themselves among his chosen people, but he is ever ready to attend to the needs of all who need his assistance. In this chapter, we will be reminded that a person's religious affiliation is often determined by an accident of birth. Consequently, the God of love includes all people with a sincere heart among his faithful. Christ's ministry of compassion was directed to all people regardless of their faith preference. By this time, the inquiring mind must be asking, 'Does this mean that a person's religious affiliation does not matter?' Hopefully this question will be thoroughly answered in the final section of this chapter.

Accident of Birth

Religion is as old as humanity and as diverse as geography. Although books on global religions usually categorise all the faiths of the world under seven or eight neat headings, the reality is that the number of religions and denominations within religions around the globe are countless. All over the world, there are tens of thousands of people groups that hold a distinct faith system dear. Religion is such an intricate part of people's lives that many are willing to die for their beliefs. Although we live in a postmodern age where the spirit of relativism has invaded most cultures, there are still some people who are inflexible when it comes to cultural ideas about God, worship and morality. We are all familiar with the faithful Sikhs and Rastafarians who refuse to uncover or cut their hair, even under government pressure. And, most recently, we have seen the extreme lengths people are prepared to go for their faith with the Muslim suicide bombers who believe that their efforts will be rewarded by a lifetime in paradise with seventy virgins. Then there are the devout Catholics who are convinced that the priest serves as the vehicle of God's forgiveness and grace. Or even the faithful Seventh-day Adventists who would rather lose their jobs than violate the sacred hours of the Sabbath. Whether or not we agree with a certain religion, we cannot deny that a measure of faith is required from everyone who calls himself religious. While most people believe that their religion is the true one, the fact that all religions make unique claims means that they cannot all be of equal validity. In spite of what many modern syncretists purport, the answer to the world's problems cannot be found in all religious systems.

Usually, a person's religion is determined by the place in which she was born. For instance, a person born in India is generally Hindu. A native of Pakistan or the Middle East is likely to be Muslim. Chinese and Korean people generally proclive towards Buddhism. The majority of you who read this book were probably born in the Western-influenced world and are consequently Christian. Nonetheless, even within Christianity the place in which a person is born often determines his denomination. An Italian, Irish or Hispanic is usually a Roman Catholic. An English person is more than likely affiliated with Anglicanism. And, until recent immigration trends, an American was customarily a member of one of many Protestant denominations such as Methodist,

Episcopalian, Quaker, or Baptist.

Since such a great variety of religions coexist, the claim that any one religion is superior to the other can sometimes seem superficial. The truth is that all of the world's religions cannot be equally true, particularly since they all make unique claims that often contradict one another. Are we saved through the sacrifice of Christ or do our good works atone for our sins? Are we all destined to be reincarnated into another life-form after death, or is all talk about an afterlife the mythical musing of primitive people? Does God require us to take pilgrimages to holy sites or can we find him in the temples of our bodies through transcendent meditation? Does marijuana open up the seeker's mind to mystical truths or are mind-altering substances an abomination to the Maker? With all these conflicting claims, how can one determine whether a certain religion is true?

On a basic level, a person accepts religious claims as truth by combining experience, faith, and reason. From a cultural perspective, every person is born into a certain religious experience and is moulded with a certain understanding of religious reality. Although many of the religious doctrines to which a person is exposed may elude general rules of science or reality — even in their own contexts — they are accepted through faith. As a person matures, she is often challenged with evaluating the experiences of others in her cultural community against the faith assertions. It is at this point of critical evaluation that the individual is compelled to determine whether or not the claims of the particular religion are reasonable. Did the world originate from a big fish, as a certain people group among the Shona of Zimbabwe believe? Or is the highest form of biological life exhibited in the cow as Hindus purport? Are we destined to endless cycles of rebirth, and is it possible that our next experience of life could be as a rodent? As absurd as these beliefs may sound to the Judeo-Christian, if any of these claims are a consistent part of a person's religious experience they accept it with the same attitude of faith that Christians exercise in the atonement of Christ. All religions make unique claims that cannot be scientifically verified, but must be embraced through the eye of faith.

Religion in the Judeo-Christian tradition makes several faith claims, the first of which is, 'In the beginning God created the heavens and the earth'. It also asserts that at the end of time, God himself will intervene in the affairs of humanity and establish an everlasting kingdom of righteousness. Further, it is punctuated by moral imperatives outlining the way in which individuals ought to relate to God and neighbour, and warns that every person will eventually have to give an account to God for actions done or undone. Particularly interesting in our religious tradition is the teaching that God selects certain individuals to be his 'chosen' people. In the Old Testament, the chosen are specifically identified as the descendants of Abraham's son Isaac and his grandson Jacob. According to the Bible, it was their responsibility to remain faithful to his demands and be agents of blessing to all the nations of the world.

Those who find these historical claims reasonable and accept them by faith, align themselves with the various sects of Judaism. Then there are others who accept all of these claims, but also believe that the descendants of Israel were superceded by a spiritual community that transcended geography and family lineage. This transferal of status was a direct result of Israel's collective failure to abide by the covenant, coupled with the rejection of Jesus of Nazareth as the Messiah of prophecy by the religious and political authorities. Those who are convinced of the central place of Jesus to the history of humanity as revealed in the Bible associate with one of the many Christian denominations.

The majority who read this book have either independently accepted the claims of Christianity or have decided to remain in Christianity because their parents or immediate circle of influence profess Christianity. Unfortunately, most of us have not challenged the claims of Christianity and have therefore not had the opportunity to exercise the kind of faith that leads to genuine acceptance, the kind of faith that can only be activated by the Holy Spirit. Sadly, many of us prefer to stay in our comfort zone of passive acceptance and feel that as long as we remain 'in the church', when Christ comes he will take us to glory with all the other nominal Christians. This passive attitude towards religion is not exclusive to Christianity, but is typical of most people around the globe for whom religion is as much a part of their cultural reality as the food they eat. They belong to a certain faith simply because everyone in their immediate community belongs to that faith. They have not taken the time to ascertain whether or not the claims made by their faith are reasonable. They are not adherents of a certain religion or denomination as a result of careful study, meditation and listening for the voice of the Spirit. Their religious affiliation is simply the byproduct of an accident of birth!

Faithful Heathens?

Jesus recognised that a person's religion and perspective of God is often due to an accident of birth, and so his mission was undiscriminating. He did not limit his works of mercy to those in the household of Israel. He recognised that salvation was not gained by family lineage or even a rational acceptance of the claims of a specific religion. Granting salvation on the grounds of family affiliation or a knowledge of certain teachings would mean that anyone who was not a member of a certain family or did not have the opportunity to investigate all religions would be automatically lost. Since people have absolutely no control over their place of birth or family of origin, and since everyone does not have the opportunity to compare beliefs with others, God alone is qualified to make the final decision about who receives salvation. Jesus powerfully demonstrated that, irrespective of one's birthplace, anyone who exercises genuine faith in God is a candidate for salvation.

The efficacy of *heathen* faith is witnessed several times in the gospels. One such incident took place when Jesus healed the slave of a Roman centurion (Matt. 8:5-13). Like many Roman soldiers, the centurion was probably an adherent of a Persian religion called Mithraism, and would have worshipped Ahura-Mazda, the god of the sun. As a distinguished officer in the imperial army, he would also have subscribed to the rituals of the imperial cult which elevated the emperor to divine status. However, the fact that he was not acquainted with the God of Israel did not make him a bad person. Mithraism promoted ethical responsibility and the civic cult helped to govern societal morality. Although their idolatrous components distanced both of these faiths from Judaism, anyone adhering to their ethical and moral demands would more than likely behave like a person who had a knowledge of God's will. This centurion was probably faithful to the light of truth that had been faintly revealed to him through his religious systems. In fact, his loving concern for others is demonstrated in the fact that he came to Jesus in behalf of one of his slaves — a piece of property. Many who have professed Christianity over the ages have viewed slaves as dispensable chattels, but this *heathen* had been possessed by a love that could only come from the God who loves the world.

In addition to his unselfish love, the centurion also expressed exemplary faith. He may not have been a Jew, but he knew there was something special about Jesus.

Although he had direct command over at least one hundred soldiers, he was willing to assume a position of humility as he reached out to the compassionate Christ for assistance. Notice the faith that he exercised in Jesus: ' "Master, I am not worthy to have you under my roof; but only say the word and my servant will be healed" ' (Matt. 8:8). Jesus did not ask to examine the man's baptismal certificate to see if he was 'a member of the church in good and regular standing'. All he knew was that a person needed his unconditional help. Impressed by the man's faith, Jesus responded: ' "Truly, I say to you, not even in Israel have I found such faith" ' (8:10). In his response, Jesus was not referring to Israel as a geographical territory, but as a religious community. It's not enough simply to possess the name of the chosen. Identity only means something if it is accompanied by action. Thrilled by the centurion's exercise of faith, Jesus further elaborated, ' "I tell you, many will come from east and west and sit at table with Abraham, Isaac, and Jacob in the kingdom of heaven, while the sons of the kingdom will be thrown into the outer darkness; there people will weep and gnash their teeth" ' (vss 11-12).

Jesus' emphasis on people coming from east and west is significant since both places were saturated with pagan mystery religions that often denied the exclusive claims of Judaism. In no uncertain terms, Jesus prophesied that many who had not even accepted the tenets of God's true religion had the ability to reach him through their faith. Indeed, this was the case with the men from the east who came to visit the baby Jesus (Matt. 2:1-12). While most translations refer to them as 'wise men', the actual Greek term used to describe them is *magoi*, from which the English word 'magic' is derived. These men were magicians or, more specifically, astrologers. As their encounter with Herod demonstrates, they were totally ignorant about

FOR GOD SO LOVED THE WORLD

the Jewish faith. Nonetheless, even in the midst of their superstition, God granted them the opportunity to have a personal encounter with the Saviour of humanity. In fact, after they had paid worshipful homage to the babe in the manger, the God of Israel personally appeared to these men in a dream and solicited their participation in the plan to protect his son (2:12).

Although the centurion and the astrologers had encountered the Christ, there is no scriptural indication that they forsook their pagan religions and embraced the religion of Israel. The same is true for the woman who approached Jesus in the district of Tyre and Sidon and begged him to heal her daughter (Matt. 15:21-28). While Mark refers to her as a Syro-Phoenecian woman, Matthew calls her a Canaanite. Matthew's choice of designation was deliberate. The very use of the term 'Canaanite' was intended to stir up deep-seated feelings of Jewish superiority and animosity towards her reckless heathenism. This woman is immediately depicted as an idolater who is so steeped in sin that she would not know how to do right, even if it were her only option! At first, it seems as if Jesus had adapted the self-righteous attitude of his compatriots. As the woman begged him for help, he totally ignored her. Assuming his distaste for this heathen woman, the disciples begged Jesus to dismiss her from their presence. Appearing to go along with their desire, Jesus remarked, ' "I was sent only to the lost sheep of the house of Israel." ' The woman would not take no for an answer and prostrated herself before Jesus and further implored him. To the disciples' glee, Jesus appeared to insult the helpless woman: ' "It is not good to take the children's food and give it to the dogs." ' With a desperate surge of faith the woman urgently retorted, ' "That is true, Master. But even the dogs eat the crumbs that fall from their masters' table." ' Having tested the woman to her limit, and probably pained by the insensitivity of the disciples and his feigned participation in their bigotry, the compassionate Christ apologetically blessed the heathen woman with the words, ' "Great is your faith! Be it done to you as you desire." '

The story ends with the healing of the woman's daughter, but Matthew is silent about the interaction between Jesus and his disciples when she was eventually dismissed. I'm sure there was a long period of thick, embarrassing silence. This would have been enough time for the disciples to take an introspective look at their attitudes. Their obvious prejudices towards the 'heathen' made it difficult for Jesus to invite the woman to become a part of his band of disciples. How would she have felt to be a part of a people who believed that her family members and neighbours were unlovable? Why should she leave her pagan system of idolatry to join a band of people who would rather see her daughter die than offer her assistance?

The attitude taken by the Jews towards the people in that region is similar to that of many modern Christians toward people of other faiths. Many forget that the privilege of being exposed to God's truth does not qualify enlightened souls for the kingdom any more than ignorance of God's will disqualifies others. Paul was very clear that the God of grace accommodated people who were unaware of his demands (Acts 17:30). Jesus was very aware that this woman was probably an idol-worshipping heathen, but he also knew that the blood he was to shed on Calvary was to suffice for the entire world, and not just a select few. Her exemplary demonstration of faith proved that she had as much right to the kingdom of heaven as the person who was nurtured in the 'truth'. His ministry of compassion to her was unconditional.

Jesus' affirmation of the validity of godly faith within

FOR GOD SO LOVED THE WORLD

other religious systems is also attested to in his inaugural sermon in Nazareth (Luke 4:24-27). In his sermon, he reminded the people in the synagogue that God has always had faithful people who were not associated with his chosen. He pointed specifically to the widow from Zarapheth in Sidon whom God appointed to assist Elijah during a divine initiated drought, and the Syrian military officer, Naaman, whom God selected for a miraculous healing. Both of these heathens put God to the test and received his blessings. Had Jesus chosen, he could also have spoken of the faith of Abimelech, the Amorite king who refused to transgress God's commandments and commit adultery; or Melchizedek, the Jebusite king who was chosen by God Almighty to bless the faithful Abraham; or Jethro, the Midianite priest who assisted Moses in organising God's people; or even Rahab, the Jerichoite who provided sanctuary for the Israelite spies.

In the account of the Good Samaritan (Luke 10:25-37), Jesus powerfully illustrates how people from other faiths are often more faithful than those who profess to honour God. The story is presented in direct response to a Jewish lawyer's question to Jesus: ' "What shall I do to inherit eternal life." ' In a style similar to Socrates, Jesus replied with another question that forced the lawyer to answer his own question: ' "All who desire to enter eternal life should display unselfish love to God and neighbour." ' Maybe the answer was too simplistic for the lawyer, and so he challenged Jesus further with the question, ' "Who is my neighbour?" ' He was probably not prepared for Jesus' response which totally radicalised the traditional rabbinical concept of the neighbour. He expected Jesus to describe the neighbour as the faithful Jew, but was shocked when Jesus placed the priest and Levite in the position of stranger, and elevated the Samaritan to neighbourly status.

This story is punctuated with the dynamics of inter-denominational prejudice. Although some scholars question the origin of the Samaritans, it is highly probable that they were the descendants of the remnant of the Northern Kingdom of Israel who had suffered defeat under Sennacherib and the Assyrians in 722 BCE. For all intents and purposes, the Samaritans and Jews were religious siblings who acknowledged the authority of the law of Moses and worshipped Yahweh. However, historical rivalries and doctrinal differences had driven them apart and, by the time of Jesus, they had a deeply entrenched hatred for each other. They each had a different view about the mountain from which God would accept worship, and had rival priesthoods and temples. As far as the Jews were concerned, the Samaritans were heretics and blasphemers and far removed from any possibility of salvation. Nonetheless, as the story of the good Samaritan informs us, when a Jew was attacked and left for dead on the road from Jerusalem to Jericho, it was not members of his own denomination who assisted him, but the rival Samaritan. Jesus ends the parable by asking, ' "Who was neighbour to the man who fell among robbers?" ' In the context of the original inquiry about the qualifications for eternal life, Jesus' question can be rephrased, 'Which of these men deserves eternal life?' This parable illustrates that it takes more than membership in a church to qualify as a *bona fide* child of God and brother or sister of the Christ. According to Jesus, ' "... [only the one who fulfills] the will of my Father in heaven is my brother, and sister, and mother" ' (Matt. 12:50). As the gospels demonstrate, these can even include faithful heathens!

The Truth about God

In this section, we will address the question that is probably on most readers' minds by now. 'Since a person's religious affiliation is heavily influenced by his place of birth, and since faithful worshippers can be found in religious systems outside of Christianity, does religious affiliation matter?' A growing number of Christian scholars propose that religious affiliation doesn't matter as they take the pluralistic view that all roads lead to heaven. Some claim it will be unfair for God to have a true religion and not make it universally accessible, while others reason that all religions are culturally-constructed myths that provide psychologically satisfying answers for life's mysteries.

However, the Bible gives a completely different picture.

While God's word is clear about the universal applicability of God's grace, it is also plain that there is only one valid way to salvation. Jesus does not mince words when he informs Thomas, ' "I am the way, the truth, and the life; no one comes to the Father except through me" ' (John 14:6). This thought is echoed by Paul who refers to the Gospel of Christ as the 'power of salvation to everyone who believes' (Rom. 1:16). Peter is also clear that there is no other name among humans 'through which we can be saved' (Acts 4:12). To place all religions on the same plain would mean falsifying the claims of Christianity. With their competing claims and conflicting world views, all religions cannot be equally valid. To make this assertion would destroy the very definition of empirical truth (unless the truth is that there is no truth — which in itself would be absurd).

Although faithful people in non-Christian religions can be just as close to the kingdom as loyal Christians, Jesus still commands his followers to evangelise the world. ' "Go," ' he says, ' "and make disciples of all nations, baptising them in the name of the Father, and of the Son, and of the Holy Spirit, and teaching them to obey everything I have commanded you" ' (Matt. 28:19-20).

One may well ask why evangelism is necessary. Why

can't faithful people experience salvation in the comfort of their familiar religious ignorance?

The answer can be found in Jesus' dialogue at the well with the Samaritan woman. When she raised the issue of true worship, Jesus reminded her that God is Spirit, and true worshippers worship him in *spirit* and *truth* (John 4:24). Faithful people in non-Christian religions may be spiritually sincere in their service to God but their zeal for worship is without knowledge. In the scheme of the great controversy between good and evil that commenced with the deception of the first couple in the Garden of Eden, *truth* matters to God. Everything that is not based on truth is a lie and proceeds from the devil.

All the people of the world must be evangelised because they need to know the *Truth* about God.

The fullness of God's revealed truth is found in his word that testifies about the uniqueness of his Son. Those who accept all the claims of God's word and acknowledge his Son as the Messiah of humanity become a part of his chosen people. While the chosen can be identified in the body of Christ, Jesus' words to his disciples must not be forgotten: ' "I have other sheep that are not of this fold; I must bring them also and they will heed my voice" ' (John 10:16). With these words, not only does Jesus confirm the existence of faithful saints in other religions, but he establishes his ultimate plan for all the faithful to be in one fold. The process of gathering all the sheep into one fold is a steady process that can only be achieved through authentic evangelistic witness. Until this happens, God's church will continue to manifest itself in two distinct ways: the *visible* church which upholds his truth, and the *invisible* church which is comprised of people from many faiths who are sincerely living up to the light that they have. The fact of an invisible church is pressed home by Paul, who enlightens us with the words, 'Whenever Gentiles, who have no knowledge of God's revealed will, instinctively do what he requires, they show that his will is embodied in their hearts, and will be judged by their sincerity' (Rom. 2:14-16). This is good news for all who are concerned about the fate of their ancestors who died in their pagan religions without receiving the opportunity to respond to the Gospel. It is also good news for the many people groups in the world today who have not yet been evangelised by genuine Christian witnesses.

While the concept of an invisible church may provide relief for those who are worried about the fate of departed loved ones, those who belong to the visible church are still under the divine commission to share God's truth with the masses. A genuine Christian witness must provide potential converts with more than their current religions offer them. They need to know that the problem with the human race is not that we are finite and God is infinite, but that we are sinners deserving death and in need of salvation. They need to know that the same God through whom the worlds were created thought so much of his creation that he transformed himself into one of us and died the death that we deserve to die so that we can live the life that only he deserves to live. They need to know that there is hope for this world that is plagued with warfare, natural disasters, starvation, and crime.

People from other faiths also need to know that their acts of piety and elaborate systems of works righteousness can do nothing to garner favour from God. My wife has a Hindu friend who recently shared with her that she had to cancel all her appointments for a day in order to undergo certain rituals for her mother-in-law who had been dead for a year. According to the belief of her particular sect of Hinduism, upon death her mother-in-law entered a state of limbo, in which she was suspended between eternal bliss and eternal damnation. It was the responsibility of her surviving sons and their families to go through elaborate rites in order to ensure her a place in paradise. For an entire year, the family of the deceased was expected to perform good deeds for other people. Additionally, once a month they were responsible for covering the expenses of a priest who had to travel a distance of a two-hundred mile round trip in order to officiate in elaborate rituals that were supposed to move the deceased to the desired place of paradise. Needless to say, these rites were costly and time consuming and there was absolutely no way of verifying if they were effective in moving the deceased from limbo.

While I am sure that my wife's friend, along with countless other Hindus, is practising her religion with all sincerity, the God who is above all does not demand such elaborate acts of piety. The compassionate Christ gently offers an invitation to all of weary humanity, ' "Come to me all who are tired and burdened, and I will relieve you. Take my yoke upon you, and learn from me because I am meek and humble in heart, and you will find relief for your souls. For my yoke is easy and my load is light" ' (Matt. 11:28-30). The Gospel of Christ is a liberating gospel that frees humans from futile efforts to control their own destinies.

Conclusion:
Anonymous Christians

We live in an ever shrinking world that continues to be divided by religion. As was mentioned in the introduction, *The Passion of the Christ* has irritated some Jewish leaders who seem to want to deny a fact of history. In retaliation, insensitive Christian leaders have renewed the unbiblical myth that the Jews are exclusively responsible for Jesus' death. Muslims and Hindus continue their squabbles in Pakistan and India. Recent world events have also opened the age old wounds between Islam and Christianity. With all the religious conflicts around the globe, it is no wonder that an increasing number of people are turning their backs on traditional religion and embracing the new religious movements informed by New Age theories, secular humanism and moral relativism. As the religions of the world compete against each other, millions of innocent children are dying from starvation, warfare is waged, diseases plague the globe, and the environment is wasting away. The world is in desperate need of permanent deliverance — the type of deliverance that not only brings unity to people, but obliterates sin and permanently restores the ecosystem. This liberation can only be found in the religion that honours the compassionate Christ.

To this cacophonous world where people are killing each other out of fear and distrust, the voice of Jesus rings clear: ' "If I be lifted up from the earth, I will draw *all* people unto me" (John 12:32). Notice his universal vision. 'I will draw *all* people unto me.' He is not concerned about their ethnicity, geographical location or current religious affiliation; he just wants them to come to him. He understands that their current faith system may be influenced by the place of their birth, and so he calls indiscriminately.

But the question remains, 'How is Christ lifted up?'

Before Jesus returned to his Father, he promised his disciples that he would send them the Holy Spirit. He knew that the Holy Spirit was the required component to break through a person's understanding of religious reality. It takes the power of God to convict a person that the path they have followed all their lives has been tainted by Satan. Through the Holy Spirit, Jesus is lifted up through transformed lives as people who once worked against God's programme become active participants in the propagation of the Gospel. God's people lift up the compassionate Christ when they allow the Holy Spirit to transform them into communities of love where unity prevails — the kind of unity that calls diverse people together under a universal umbrella to protect them from the acid rain of this evil age.

These communities of love lift up Christ when they offer refuge for the persecuted, and in the spirit of Christ embrace all people unconditionally. They lift up Christ when they model the type of love that doesn't view people of other faiths as heathens bound for hell, but as children of God who are in temporary human-made shelters as they try to find their way home to Christ's eternal mansion.

As we follow the compassionate ministry of Christ, we should be the guides to lead them there. As we seek out the faithful heathens, whom theologian Karl Rahner describes as 'anonymous Christians,' let's go with the conviction that 'God loved the *world* so much, that he gave his only born son, so that *whoever* believes in him should not perish but have eternal life' (John 3:16).

Reflect

1. Can non-Christians be saved without accepting Christ? If so, why evangelise? If not, what hope do they have?
2. There has been a recent wave of suicide bombings by Muslim martyrs who believe they will be guaranteed a place in paradise. Can God reward the faith of these suicide bombers with eternal life?
3. When compared to other religions with which you are familiar, what are the advantages of Christianity?
4. What role does the Holy Spirit play in leading a person to Christ?

Apply

1. Consult an encyclopedia and learn something about three religions or denominations you currently know nothing about.
2. Think of five questions that can help to arouse a secular person's interest in Christianity.
3. Without using the Bible, how would you share the Gospel of Christ with a Muslim, Hindu, or Buddhist?
4. List five things that can be changed in your church service that will make Christianity more appealing to non-believers.

Chapter 3
Neither do I condemn you

'After he stood, Jesus said to her, "Woman, where are they? Has no one condemned you?" And the woman said, "No one, Lord." Then Jesus said, "Neither do I condemn you; go, and from now on stop living a life of sin." '
John 8:10-11.

Some religious critics of *The Passion of the Christ* question whether Mel Gibson is spiritually qualified to make a movie about the central figure of Christianity. Although Gibson is associated with a conservative faction of the Catholic Church, his sincerity has been challenged by those who cannot harmonise his professed desire to spread the Gospel, with his promotion of extreme violence in movies like *Braveheart* or *Lethal Weapon*. Most religious leaders overlooked the dissonance and embraced the movie for evangelistic purposes. Conservative evangelicals who vehemently disapproved of the rampant immorality coming from Hollywood, embraced Gibson as the temporary successor of Billy Graham! Indeed, it was largely the support of Christians that catapulted box office sales to hundreds of millions of dollars in less than a month, turning *The Passion of the Christ* into one of the most successful projects in the history of film.

As I witness the surge of interest in Christianity evoked by Gibson's portrayal of the final hours of Jesus' life, and hear the testimonies of people who claim conversion from their visual encounter, I wonder how Jesus feels? Is he touched by the fact that Gibson invested over thirty-five-million dollars from his personal resources to make this movie even after all the major studios in Hollywood had turned him down? Is he pleased that people are being confronted with the story of salvation in a unique and unusual way? Is he able to overlook the overtly Catholic propaganda in a movie that elevates Mary as an agent of forgiveness? Is he bothered that people may leave the theatres with the erroneous impression that our sins were atoned for by Christ's torturous suffering and not by his death?

Gibson may not be a poster child for biblical Christianity, and is even affiliated with a sect of Christianity that is heavily saturated with pagan rituals, but he risked personal wealth and reputation when he embarked on a labour of love in honour of the God he professes. Does this act of service mean that Mel Gibson has a guaranteed condominium in the Kingdom of Heaven? Can he go back to making movies that promote irresponsible violence, vulgar language and sexual immorality? Does the blood of the Christ who accepts sincere offerings — however tainted they may be — cover wilful acts of rebellion after a person has been absolved of confessed sin? More importantly, who has the right to determine whether a person is worthy of salvation? Since all have sinned and fallen short of God's glory, isn't it the epitome of hypocrisy to condemn others for their hypocrisy? Shouldn't the church of God just focus on bringing people in rather than finding ways to keep people out? These and other questions will be answered in this chapter as we examine the limits and purpose of Christ's compassion for others within and outside the church.

A Safe Place

Why would millions of people pay to see a movie about Jesus, but refuse to enter a church? Could it be that when individuals attend the cinema they know they will not be judged by self-righteous members? There is no real decorum for the cinema. People can come in a tuxedo if they so desire, or they can wear jeans and t-shirts. The cinema is also a place of social integration. Nobody cares if the person sitting on the same row is black or white, young or old, gay or straight, divorced or single, ex-convict or police officer, or a stockbroker or factory worker. The only rule of the cinema is that you allow the other person to watch the movie unhindered. At the completion of the movie, they have all shared a collective experience in a non-threatening environment and leave the place changed by the message.

What would happen if that same person attended your church to learn about Jesus? If the person dared to come in jeans and sneakers, would she make it past the deacons? Would she get an insensitively charged, demeaning lecture about giving her best to God? Or would the more compassionate Pharisees take her to the musky closet in the back and cajole her to change into the Victorian clothes donated to the church by an elderly member? And let's not attempt to justify some of those other churches that pride themselves in being 'seeker friendly'. Sometimes the only seeker they are friendly towards is that person in the sneakers and jeans; and the tuxedo wearing visitor who was simply looking for a place to offer quiet praise is snubbed as a bourgeois capitalist pig!

Or what would happen if a person came to your church who did not fit into the social culture? Even as cosmopolitan societies in the world edge into an era of racial tolerance and intermarriage, many churches still fight to keep their ethnic identities. As secular sinners embrace the wisdom of forming partnerships across racial lines, the church remains the most segregated institution in society. The same people who sat next to each other in the cinema would not be welcome in the other's church. We can work and play together, but worshipping and praying together is completely out of the question. We have become so comfortable with segregation, that we have even developed arguments to pacify our cognitive dissonance. The most common argument concerns the perceived discomfort of a person attending a church dominated by a certain ethnic group. We don't think of ways to alleviate the discomfort, but resolve in our minds that we are unable to create a welcoming environment. We'll just cater to our 'own' people. If Mr English wants to learn about Jesus, let him find an Anglo church. If Mr Guyana needs salvation, let him find an Afro church. If Mr China is interested in heaven, let him find an Asian church. We can all go to the same place to see *The Passion of the Christ*, but let's not even think about multicultural places of worship!

Perhaps the people who are least welcome in the church are those who have been labelled with a certain sin. Some categories of sinners are warmly received in many churches. Not many are appalled by the gossipers, the backbiters, the proud, the selfish, the adulterers, and those involved in other 'acceptable' sins. However, other sinners are definitely not welcome in most churches. If the neighbourhood alcoholic visits on the day of communion we automatically assume that he must have mistaken our church for one that uses real wine! Or if a recently divorced woman attends a church social, the sisters make her feel like a lady of the night as they jealously guard their husbands. And don't let a homosexual step foot on the church grounds – all of a sudden the church begins to smell like a hospital as insensitive ushers sanitise everywhere he touches in their desperate bid to stop the spread of AIDS!

These examples are deliberately exaggerated and it would be unfair to categorise all congregations as unfriendly, meanspirited people, but few can deny that many societal outcasts feel that the church despises them. For many, the church is not a 'safe place' but a house of guilt. They don't view the church as a place where their burdens can be lifted, but avoid it in fear that church attendance will increase the weight of the sins that they carry around. Most feel too dirty to come to church, and in a spirit of destructive submission have condemned themselves.

So far, we have drawn negative comparisons between the acceptance people tend to experience at the cinema and the church. However, there are some other important factors that must be considered. While the cinema is a place where diverse people can come and sit together in close proximity, it has a completely different function from a church. Very little human interaction takes place and in many ways the darkened environment does not help to foster an atmosphere for socialising. It is a place of assembly, but it can hardly qualify as a meeting place where people are enriched by meaningful conversation and touched by random acts of kindness. In the impersonal atmosphere of the cinema, people can maintain their anonymity and are under no pressure to make themselves vulnerable to others who may be able to assist them with their problems. The only thing people in the cinema have in common is the desire to see a movie. They are not concerned about the social welfare of the other individuals sitting on their row, but are only in attendance for the purpose of self-amusement.

It is precisely because God *is* concerned about the welfare of sinners that he has entrusted to individuals who are called by his name the task of caring about the eternal destiny of others. While we may be tempted to leave blatant sinners to reap the destruction of their deviant actions, Peter reminds us that God 'is not willing that any should perish, but that all should come to repentance' (2 Peter 3:9). Although it is easy to support the death penalty for murderers, paedophiles, and serial rapists, John cautions us that 'God did not send his Son into the world to condemn it, but to save it' (John 3:17). If universal salvation is God's desire, then his church should be about the business of providing safe places where sinners can find refuge and transformation.

Benefit of the Doubt
In the Gospels, Christ himself has provided several examples of how to relate to sinners in need of safety. Probably the most notable story is the one of the woman caught in the act of adultery (John 8:2-11). While some scholars identify the woman with one of the Marys who followed Jesus, the Bible does not give her a name. Interestingly, the account took place soon after Jesus had invited the spiritually thirsty to come to him for refreshment (7:37-38). Although she was obviously in need of the Holy Spirit, this adulterous woman did not voluntarily come to Jesus in response to his altar call. She was forcefully dragged before him by Pharisees thirsting for blood under the guise of justice. There was no question about the woman's guilt. The text is plain that she was caught 'in the very act of adultery'. She had violated the law of God, and the scripture was plain that her punishment should be death by stoning. There were no extenuating circumstances that could lead to her acquittal. She was not a victim of rape or an adventurous teenager who got drunk with a high school date. She was a married woman who was romantically involved with a man to whom she was not married. The woman was a sin-

ner who had brought disgrace on her home, her religion, her nation and her God.

As one who had affirmed that it was not his intention to destroy the law, Jesus could have endorsed the death sentence. However, the text says that when enticed by the scribes and Pharisees to provide an opinion on the punishment stipulated by Moses, Jesus simply stooped and began to write on the ground with his finger. The frustrated scribes and Pharisees persisted in their attempt to lure Jesus into joining their dastardly deed, but Jesus kept silent. Eventually, when he tired of their constant coaxing for him to adjudicate the case, he simply stood up and challenged the crowd: ' "The one who is sinless among you, let him be the first to throw a stone at her" ' (8:7b). After uttering these damning words, he resumed his position and continued writing on the ground.

The Bible does not tell us what Jesus wrote, but it wouldn't be surprising if he simply rewrote the Ten Commandments, knowing that 'all have sinned and consequently lack God's glory' (Rom. 3:23). Obviously the written and spoken words of Jesus impressed the mob of their own sinfulness, for each of the men walked away without so much as throwing a pebble. The woman was probably huddled in a ball with her head covered, petrified at the thought of her impending doom and bracing her body for the barrage of stone missiles. She heard the words of Jesus and probably wondered what all the shuffling was about. Surely the righteous men who had exposed her filth had no skeletons in *their* closets.

After a terrifying period of silence, her heart probably picked up the pace at the sound of Jesus' question to the nameless sinner, 'Woman where are they? Has no one condemned you?' Sheepishly releasing herself from her cowering foetal position, the woman must have slowly lifted her head and looked around. To her surprise, the only person left was Jesus. Finally, in response to his question, she whispered, 'No one has condemned me, Lord.' But deep in her heart she must have wondered why Jesus was still there. The others had left because they were guilty of sin, but Jesus' presence meant that he was perfect. They did not have the moral right to stone her, but Jesus did. Could this be a cruel trick? Was Jesus going to get the satisfaction of stoning her all by himself? Sensing her need for relief, Jesus provided her with the most refreshing words she had ever heard in her life, 'Neither do I condemn you; go, and from this moment don't continue to sin.'

What conclusions can be drawn from Jesus' handling of the situation? Was he saying that nobody has the right to cast judgement on another? Was he implying that anyone who wishes can be baptised without showing evidence of genuine repentance? Was he putting an end to church discipline and laying the ground for all people to find membership in the church, regardless of lifestyle? Does this passage give precedent for the growing number of homosexuals in Christian churches to practise their sinful lifestyles without fear of censorship? Does the pardoning of this woman, who was undoubtedly in violation of God's law, give us all the excuse to 'sin boldly' and presume on God's forgiveness? Does it give Mel Gibson an excuse to make more movies that desensitise people to mindless violence? Does it provide progressive pastors with an excuse to distribute condoms to prostitutes and clean needles to crack addicts?

I submit that all of the preceding questions must be answered with an emphatic *no!* Before anyone thinks that this passage can be used as a platform for licentious Christianity, three very important factors ought to be considered. First is the motive of the men who brought the woman to Jesus. It is easily apparent that they were not really concerned about justice. They purported that the woman was caught 'in the very act of adultery'. If this were the case, then there should have been *two* people in the court of popular vengeance. However, they were so bigoted and chauvinistically blinded that they took the weaker party and excused the man. In an environment where justice is laden with prejudice, there are always going to be problems. How can a church vote to drop a young lady from the books because she became pregnant outside of wedlock, but does nothing to the pastor's son who sexually harasses all the females in his youth group? How can a church censor a person for going to prison for an unpaid traffic violation, but does nothing about the malicious gossiping that is tearing the membership apart? How can a church deny the request of Alcoholics Anonymous to hold meetings in the youth hall when half of its own membership is struggling with various types of addiction? There is nothing wrong with holding people accountable for their actions, but those who assume the responsibility must do so with sensitivity and impartiality.

The second factor to be considered in this story is the spiritual status of the men who brought the adulterous woman to Jesus. The fact that their motives were wrong is evidence enough that they were spiritually delinquent. Those who are filled with the Spirit know that the person caught in a sin is not to be condemned by her siblings but restored. When Joseph discovered that Mary was pregnant with Jesus, he had all legal rights to demand that she be stoned. Although they were only engaged, Jewish law held that their commitment was as binding as marriage. However, rather than follow the letter of the law, 'Joseph, being a righteous man, did not wish to expose her to public shame, but sought secretly to divorce her' (Matt. 1:19).

Spiritual people are sensitive and spiritually attuned to the will of God. They are not quick to inflict vengeance but are patient in mercy. The scribes and Pharisees who brought the woman to Jesus did not have this spirit, and when Jesus wrote on the ground they became convicted of their own sinfulness. They realised that they were not in the position to punish this sinner because they themselves were sinners – they were not in the right spiritual condition to administer discipline.

The third factor to be considered in this passage is Jesus' admonition to the woman: 'Go, and from this moment don't continue to sin.' In no uncertain terms, Jesus let her know that he did not endorse her behaviour. He recognised that she was in violation of the law of God. He recognised that she was worthy of death. The scribes and Pharisees did not bring her to the temple on trumped up charges. She *was* guilty. But so was every one of the men who had brought her to him. It is in this light that Jesus extended the grace of God to this frightened and repentant woman – the same grace that was available to each of her accusers. With his tender act of mercy, Jesus gave the guilty woman a second chance to make it right with her Maker. In challenging the woman to avoid a life of sin, Jesus assured her that she had the ability to live a life of victory. He was probably aware that she would face difficult moments at home when the town gossipers informed her husband about her unfaithful actions that day. She may even have had a strong emotional attachment to her lover and would have to pray continuously when her mind wandered into forbidden areas of lustful fantasy. But the compassionate Christ had placed his trust in her and boosted her confidence when he challenged her to make godly choices in life.

The Bible does not tell us what happened to this woman. Maybe she was so transformed by her 'near death experience' that she immediately broke off the relationship with her paramour and took the initiative in mending the broken relationship with her husband. Or she may have gone home and confessed to her husband who refused to forgive her and had her stoned to death anyhow. In another possible scenario, she could have run back to the arms of her lover and planned new secretive strategies to ensure the longevity of their sordid relationship. Whatever path she chose to take, the compassionate Christ had given her the benefit of the doubt, and it was up to her to take advantage of his grace.

Go and Sin No More

While we cannot know the woman's decision, there are several known people in the Gospels who took advantage of the second chance afforded them by Jesus. Although she is only mentioned once before the crucifixion and resurrection (Luke 8:2), the mysterious Mary Magdalene is often depicted as one of Jesus' most loyal followers. Before her encounter with Jesus, she had been possessed by seven demons. Usually, when we think of demon possession, we picture people frothing at the mouth with their eyes rolling, speaking in different voices and committing slow and painful serial murders. However, most forms of demon possession are more sophisticated. Corporate executives who pay themselves hundreds of millions of dollars a year while 'downsizing' the workforce by terminating thousands of jobs are, arguably, demon oppressed. So are gutless pimps who entice fatherless and love-starved teenagers to sell their bodies to lust-filled strangers. So are media personalities who make a living promoting godless immorality. So are directionless teenagers who roam the street looking for the next opportunity to vandalise or terrorise. So are leaders of nations who have no respect for human life and treat their armies as dispensable chess pieces. So are hat wearing deaconesses who put on their best clothes for church but spend the rest of the week as channels of gossip. So are stiff-suited elders who display an air of respectability but spend their days plotting to overthrow the pastor. Given its many faces, we cannot be sure about the exact nature of Mary's demon possession, but we can be sure that it had separated her from God.

It was only Jesus' willingness to show compassion to Mary that enabled her to be free from her demons. The people in the church probably felt she was beyond redemption. I'm sure they assumed that God had left her to wallow in her own reprobate state. However, Jesus looked beyond her situation and saw her potential as he not only healed her, but invited her to become a follower.

Because she had been shown love when others thought her unlovable, Mary Magdalene devoted the rest of her days to Jesus. While the Bible does not stipulate, many believe that like Mary, the sister of Martha, in John's Gospel, Mary Magdalene was the unnamed woman who anointed Jesus with expensive perfume in the Gospels of Matthew, Mark and Luke. Whatever the case, Mary proved herself to be a faithful follower, and while the male disciples were hiding in fear for their lives, Mary Magdalene was among the faithful few to witness the crucifixion, and was also among the first to visit the tomb on resurrection morning. Mary is a powerful witness to the potency of the Spirit as she serves as a constant reminder to the body of Christ that even those who are involved in the most heinous sins are within the reach of salvation.

Zacchaeus is another example of the many who were transformed as a result of their encounter with Jesus (Luke 19:1-10). The text reveals that he was a very wealthy individual who had risen to the position of Chief Executive

Officer of the tax collection agency. As the account unfolds, we learn that his rise to the top was probably not based on his merit but on extortion and deception. He was not only powerful but corrupt. As a Jew working for the Roman government, there is little doubt that he had given up on his ancestral faith. In many ways he was like the Prodigal Son who had wandered far from home. There is no doubt that Zacchaeus was hated by his compatriots. When the civic events were planned to honour those who had done well from the community, Zacchaeus' name never made it to the list. He was always going to carry the stigma of *persona non grata*.

Like many corporate executives today, Zacchaeus may have been saturated in wealth, and may even have had direct access to the emperor and other powerful people in the Roman Senate; but he was unfulfilled. He felt that money could buy him happiness but, after investing in real estate and luxury goods, he still had the same yearning in his soul as the crack addict looking for the next fix. He had probably thought about returning to church many times. However, each time he passed a church member in the market he was snubbed. It seems as if the only time the church had any interest in him was when they wanted a donation for missions or a new building. He felt used by the church and for years had no problem playing the role of the cutthroat business mogul. But now, the Holy Spirit had started speaking to his heart and he was just waiting for a person of God to approach him and invite him to make a decision. He was a fruit ripe for the picking, but the ecclesiastical establishment had written him off.

Zacchaeus' desperation is evidenced in the risks that he took to get a glimpse of Jesus. He was taking a big chance by just being in a crowd with people who would have killed him with no remorse. But he had to see Jesus. So serious was he, that he forgot about pride and reputation and coaxed his middle-aged bones and sinews to assist him in climbing a sycamore tree. Perhaps Mel Gibson's effort to produce this movie about Jesus was *his* sycamore tree experience. And who can tell whether Bill Gates's billion dollar grant to fight AIDS in Africa was his attempt to climb the sycamore tree? I wonder how many church leaders encouraged their members to write letters of appreciation to the Bill Gates foundation for this act of charity? I wonder how many heads of churches paid him a 'no strings attached' visit to express personal appreciation for his philanthropy? While it is necessary to hold the wealthy accountable when they exploit and oppress, I wonder what would happen if the church started commending their philanthropic efforts.

The compassionate Christ definitely noticed Zacchaeus' efforts and called to him in the tree, 'Hurry up and come down, because I'm going to be a guest in your house.' The people were probably surprised when the person clumsily made his way down the tree and pulled the shawl from his head, thus revealing the familiar face of the man everybody loved to hate. This was the notorious Zacchaeus. Did Jesus know what he does for a living? Could Jesus really be inviting himself to this sinner's house? Jesus was very aware of all these things, but apparently wanted to make a statement. He could have secretly asked a disciple to deliver a message to Zacchaeus. However, by exposing Zacchaeus he afforded him the opportunity to confess publically and express his repentance to the people who had been hurt by his actions. Who knows how many years Zacchaeus had been waiting for an opportunity to perform these acts of kindness and restoration? All he needed was a person of God who cared about him enough to treat him like a fellow human being.

Jesus' final words to the crowd are significant: ' "Today salvation has come to this house, for this man is *also* a son of Abraham. The son of man has come to seek and to save the lost" ' (Luke 19:9-10). The church may have written him off, but Zacchaeus was as much a 'son of Abraham' as the rest. This wealthy plutocrat needed to be rescued as much as the common thief. Jesus came to seek out and save all who are 'lost'. Interestingly, the word translated lost is better translated 'totally lost' or 'beyond repair'. The church had consigned Zacchaeus to the trash heap but Jesus was willing to sift through the filth and redeem him. Although he had slumped into the depths of sin, God still had a plan for his life. Thankfully, Zacchaeus embraced God's plan as he responded positively to the compassion of the Christ.

Jesus and a Blue Collar Worker
Perhaps the best example of the fruit of Christ's compassion is seen in his relationship with Peter. When we are first introduced to Peter he is working in a fishing business with his brother Andrew. There is no indication that he was particularly religious. He was not a priest, scribe or a rabbi – just an ordinary man. Peter was probably the typical blue collar worker who worked hard during the day, and visited the local pub in the evening for a game of darts and a pint of Palestinian lager. On the weekends, he would probably attend his favourite sports event, have a laugh with the lads and then prepare for the same cycle again in the coming week. His mundane cycle was broken when Jesus approached him and appealed to his adventurous spirit. In many ways, Peter was like the person who was tired of the same routine in life and decided to give the church a try after impulsively visiting an evangelistic meeting.

Not being an overtly religious person, Peter had a lot to learn about what it meant to be a follower of Christ. He was a special case who needed extra patience and careful attention. Maybe this is the reason why Jesus kept him in his inner circle along with James and John (who had probably earned their 'sons of thunder' nickname!). Peter was rough around the edges, but he had great potential. Like many new converts, he was excited about the message and wanted to see the kingdom inaugurated as soon as possible. When Jesus asked the disciples to declare his true identity, it was Peter who blurted out, ' "You are the Christ, the Son of the living God" ' (Matt. 16:16). It was also Peter who challenged Jesus when he prophesied that the disciples would desert him. ' "They may be ashamed of you," ' Peter demeaned his colleagues, ' "But I will *never* be ashamed" ' (26:33). Indeed, when Jesus was arrested in Gethsemane, Peter demonstrated his seriousness by drawing his illegal sword and severing the ear of Malchus, the servant of the high priest (John 18:10). Unfortunately, it was the same zealous Peter who eventually caved in under pressure as he denied Christ and, subsequently, coaxed the other disciples to join his fishing business (21:1-4).

Similar to Peter, many converts to the church begin their Christian walk with zeal and seem as if they will never tire. Proud of their new status, they share the Gospel with anyone who will listen. When others who joined the church at the same time as they did get discouraged and leave, they promise the Saviour that *they* will never desert him. Then disappointments begin to plague their lives. The pastor forgets to follow up on their request for him to give Bible studies to a neighbour. Their supervisor wants them to come into work on the weekends during Sabbath hours. They find out that the local elder is having an affair with the church secretary. All of a sudden, their world falls apart and they decide that they will return to fishing. They stop coming to church, and know that they made the right decision when after a month of non-attendance they have not received a single call or visit from a concerned member. Meanwhile, back at the church some of the self-righteous Pharisees, who happened to notice that the new believers did not show up for a few services, begin to cash in on the bets they had made about the initial sincerity of the converts' decision.

We can thank God that the compassionate Christ did not give up on Peter. While Peter led the disciples in a failed fishing expedition, Jesus showed up on the coast and helped to restore his faith (John 21:1-19). After cooking a sumptuous breakfast of roast fish and bread for the disciples, Jesus focused his attention on the backslidden Peter. Addressing him by his full name like a parent reprimanding a child, Jesus asked Peter, ' "Simon, son of John, do you *love* me more than these?" ' Scholars are divided over the exact meaning of 'these'. Some feel that Jesus could have been pointing at an uncooked fish as he asked the question, and was really asking him to choose between his fishing business and discipleship. Another view, which is preferred, is that Jesus was challenging Peter to compare his love with the love of the other disciples. Did the one who ran away in fear after promising Jesus that he would never desert or deny him have more love for his Saviour than the others?

Peter responded, 'Indeed Lord; you know that I *love* you.' Most Bible versions fail to convey the full sense of Peter's response to Jesus. Firstly, while the Greek word used to preface Peter's reply can be translated 'yes', it is better rendered in this situation as 'indeed' or 'certainly'. Secondly, the false impression is given that Peter reflected the exact words of Jesus, when he professed that he *loved* him. However, the full dynamic of the conversation is only realised when it is noticed that Jesus asked Peter whether he had an *agapë* type love for him, and Peter could only admit to having the *philë* brand of love – a familial type of love shared between friends or siblings. *Agapë* love is durable, stable and unconditional, but Peter had deserted his friend at an hour when he was needed the most. Knowing his failure, he could not admit to having a weatherproof love, but he did love him as a friend (*philë*). He may not have been there at the crucifixion, but he did show up at the tomb on Sunday morning. Looking past Peter's obvious defects, Jesus locked eyes with the embarrassed backslider and charged him, 'Feed my lambs'. Jesus had seen Peter's earlier zeal and commitment, and knew he was an essential part of the team. He has suffered a momentary lapse into the pit of discouragement, but this did not mean that his days of service were over.

As if subtly reminding Peter of the number of times he had denied him, Jesus questioned Peter's love twice more and gave him a similar charge. Interestingly, the third time around, Jesus interrogated him by asking, 'Simon, son of John, do you have *philë* for me?' The Bible informs us that Peter was terribly hurt by Jesus' question. However, it was a necessary question. It's not that Jesus doubted Peter's friendship, but he wanted Peter to evaluate the true meaning of friendship. Circumstances may cause obstacles to come between two people in a relationship, but a true friend knows that any obstacle can be surmounted when people are committed to each other. Peter should not have felt that his only option was to go back to fishing after he had backslidden, he should have known that the compassionate Christ was willing to extend full forgiveness to him. Following restoration, Peter became a mighty evangelist for Jesus and would eventually die a martyr's death.

Conclusion:
Wisdom is Justified by Her Children

These success stories let us know that it is possible for people who are shown compassion to be completely regenerated. Sometimes when people of the church take seriously the charge to 'rescue the perishing and care for the dying' they will open themselves up to criticism. People may not understand why a church of God that agrees to sponsor an Alcoholics Anonymous programme will allow the recovering alcoholics to drink caffeinated beverages on the church premises. Some may decry a youth pastor's pioneering attempt to start a Christian club for the neighbourhood youth complete with a non-alcoholic bar, dance floor and wholesome upbeat music with positive lyrics. Others will question the sexuality of the young man who targets a gay bar for his place of ministry. A mother who provides temporary refuge for pregnant or runaway teenage girls may even be seen as encouraging promiscuity and delinquency. However, as long as these actions are being done with the compassion of the Christ, with the purpose of restoring his image in the hearts of estranged individuals, they are being done to the glory of God.

Jesus himself was subject to criticism when he exercised compassion to the outcasts. They accused him of being an intemperate drunkard who hung out with the wrong type of people. His only response to his critics was, 'wisdom is justified by her children' (Matt. 11:19). In other words, he was asking them to look at the fruit of his ministry. Look at the serial-polygamous and blatantly adulterous woman at the well, who drank from the water of life and became an evangelist for her entire Samaritan village. Look at Mary Magdalene, who had seven demons cast out of her and was transformed into a model citizen with pride and integrity. Look at Zacchaeus, who had spent his days in extortion and oppression but became the biggest philanthropist in Palestine. Look at Peter, who was stuck in a rut but found that his life could be meaningful if he invested it in seeking the salvation of others. Look at the criminal, who was sentenced to death by crucifixion for rampant crimes against humanity but accepted the blood of Jesus and became a paradigm of hope for the most dreadful criminals facing capital punishment on death row. Alternative methods of reaching people with the Gospel may not be in the denominational handbook, but 'wisdom is justified by her children'.

Wisdom must also be exercised in dealing with erring members within the church. Had Jesus not exercised patience with Peter, who would have preached the powerful sermon on the day of Pentecost? Who would have received the vision that opened the door to Gentile evangelism? Who would have said to the lame beggar, 'In the name of Jesus, get up and walk'? Whose shadow would have provided the source of healing for the scores of sick people? While the church must definitely ensure that the members live faithful lives of righteousness, it is not the church's business to execute God's work of final judgement. Don't get me wrong, sometimes it is necessary for the church to discipline members who, by their persistent sinful actions, demonstrate that they really don't desire to be a part of the church (Matt. 18:15-17; 1 Cor. 5:1-13). However, the first course of action towards church members who have fallen victim to Satan's snare should always be restoration (Gal. 6:1-3).

In dealing with sinners both inside and outside the community of faith, the law of Christ must always be the controlling factor. The final appeal in scripture comes in the form of a universal invitation: 'The Spirit and the bride say, "Come." And let the one who is hearing say, "Come." And the one who thirsts, let him come, the one who desires let him take freely the water of life' (Rev. 22:17). This is not just an invitation to the thirsty, it is an invitation for those who have found the source of water to join the Spirit and the bride in inviting others to drink. As the tremendous response to *The Passion of the Christ* has demonstrated, there are millions of thirsty people in the world. Will you join Jesus' ministry of compassion and let them know that they can be free from sin and its consequences? Will you let the prisoner of sin know that there is 'no condemnation for those who are in Christ Jesus' (Rom. 8:1)?

Reflect

1. What is the purpose of God's church in the world?
2. Are there limits to the compassion that should be extended to non-believers?
3. Since we are all sinners, does anybody really have the right to judge whether another person is good or bad?
4. How does your church deal with members who have sinned?

Apply

1. List five things that can be done to ensure that your place of worship provides a welcoming environment for different ethnic groups.
2. Think of a way to show compassion to a person who has been hurt by a church or a fellow Christian.
3. Encourage your pastor and church siblings to write letters of appreciation to the Bill Gates Foundation for their charitable donation to fight AIDS in Africa.
4. Consult Matthew 18:15-17, 1 Corinthians 5:1-13 and Galatians 6:1-3, and develop a biblical outline for relating to church members who have erred.

Chapter 4
Do you want to be healed?

'And Jesus went about all the cities and villages teaching in the synagogues and preaching the gospel of the kingdom and healing every disease and every ailment.'
Matthew 9:35.

By his own admission, Mel Gibson's major goal in *The Passion of the Christ* was to impress the extent of Jesus' physical suffering upon viewers. Taking advantage of his cinematic licence, Gibson embellished the biblical record to such an extent that by the time the various groups had finished abusing Jesus, there was hardly a square millimetre on his body that had not been battered, bruised, or bloodied. Indeed, it was the badly beaten corpse that was eventually put to rest in the borrowed tomb. With the repetition of violence throughout the movie, viewers were probably too numb to appreciate Jesus' totally restored body after the resurrection.

While it is necessary for Christians to contemplate Christ's suffering, it is also important to remember that he came to the earth to *relieve* suffering. There are many devout people who spend hours meditating on various aspect of Jesus' life and constructing theological arguments to explain mysteries understood only to the heavenly court. However, Jesus is better honoured when people emulate his desire to alleviate hurt and pain. As we peruse the Gospels, nowhere is his concern for the afflicted more evident than in his ministry of healing. In the first chapter, we learned that one of the tenets of Jesus' ministry involved the 'recovering of sight to the blind'. In all likelihood, this phrase was intended to be a general reference to his healing ministry which was an essential part of his mission.

In a powerful way, Jesus' ministry of healing provided practical proof that the kingdom of Satan had fallen. He could have told many parables about the kingdom, but at the end of the day he would have appeared no different from the Buddhist teacher Gautama or the Bahai's Bahaullah. However, the healing miracles set him apart from other great teachers as they demonstrated God's ability to reverse the curse of sin. The many acts of healing gave the assurance that debilitating illnesses, viruses and other ailments do not have to be a part of the human experience. Jesus knew that ultimate healing for all of humanity would not take place until the New Jerusalem is established, when the words 'sickness', 'death', and 'pain' will be eternally erased from the dictionary. However, until the manifestation of the kingdom, Jesus believed it his purpose to offer the suffering and their support group a foretaste of heaven. Through the compassionate work of his Son, the God who loves the world and its inhabitants provided tangible proof of his desire for human wholeness.

Faith and Healing

The book of Hebrews describes faith as 'the assurance of things hoped for, the evidence of things *that cannot be seen*' (Heb. 11:1). Indeed, all who believe in the Kingdom of God can only embrace it through the eyes of faith. None has seen any of the buildings in the kingdom, and it is impossible to fathom living forever and never getting old, weak or sick. It is difficult to imagine travelling at the speed of thought! Knowing how hard it is for people to see beyond their limited human experience, Jesus' healing ministry was intended to awaken the people to spiritual reality. If we can see beyond our limited scope of vision, we can step into a world of new realities. Each person who experienced Jesus' healing touch first had to visualise himself in a renewed state.

While Jesus was the one through whom healing miracles were effected, the success of the healing also depended on the participation of another. Either the person requiring healing or someone close to him or her had to exercise the faith that healing was possible. There is not a single incident of healing in the Gospels in which faith was not demanded. One of the first recorded healing miracles in Luke's Gospel involved the restoration of Peter's mother-in-law (Luke 4:38-39). This event took place on a Sabbath after Jesus had preached in the local synagogue at Capernaum and exorcised a demon possessed man. After an exhausting day, the men went to their lodgings expecting a refreshing meal. They were saddened to find Peter's mother-in-law in such a helpless state. Instead of panicking, Jesus laid his compassionate hands on her and commanded the sickness to leave. It was then the responsibility of Peter's mother-in-law to respond in faith. Visualising herself as whole, she didn't even ask anyone to get her a glass of water to assist in her recuperation, instead she 'immediately' got up and served up a sumptuous meal as if she had merely been resting.

The necessity of faith is also seen with the man who sat by the pool of Bethesda, waiting for an angel to disturb it so that he could throw himself in and be healed (John 5:1-18). Although the Bible doesn't describe the nature of his illness, many believe that he was paralysed. Whatever his ailment, he was obviously restricted in movement. When Jesus met him on that blessed Sabbath day, all he said was, 'Arise, take up your bed and walk.' The man could have entered into a debate with Jesus about his lethargic condition and the absurdity of the command. As the passage reveals later, he didn't even know who Jesus was. However, as he looked into the compassionate eyes of the mighty healer, he responded in faith and defied his atrophied muscles and ignored his brittle bones. As faith met faith, this man who had been immobile for thirty-eight years stood up, picked up his bed and walked.

This type of faith was also effective in enabling orthopaedic surgery. All of the Synoptic Gospels contain the story of the man with the withered hand whom Jesus encountered in the synagogue one Sabbath (Matt. 12:9-14; Mark 3:1-6; Luke 6:6-11). As far as the doctors were concerned, this man could not even be healed with reconstructive surgery. The only way he could gain any semblance of mobility was with the addition of a prosthetic arm. However, when Jesus told him to stretch out his deteriorated hand, the man defied physical limitations and immediately witnessed his bad hand being transformed to wholeness. At last he could lift his hands and praise the Lord!

Another orthopaedic success story involved the woman with the bent-over back (Luke 13:10-17). She probably attended synagogue faithfully every week, but could not even sit with the worshippers because of her condition. But when Jesus saw her, he was moved to lay his hand upon her back and did what the chiropractors thought impossible. The woman was instantly restored and immediately praised God. Although the text does not stipulate the nature of her praise, it would probably not be a stretch of the imagination to visualise her engaged in a holy dance and shouting 'Hallelujah!' at the top of her voice. When the Pharisees accused Jesus of violating the fourth commandment, he simply responded, 'Shouldn't this daughter of Abraham, who has been bound by the deceiver for eighteen years, be loosed from this prison on the Sabbath day?' Because healing is an indication that the devil does not have ultimate control, there is no better day than the Sabbath for a person to experience healing. This is not to say that Jesus did not perform his ministry of healing throughout the week. He did not believe that acts of mercy should be limited to that one day a week when church people find it convenient to visit sick people in the hospital. Jesus was concerned with the restoration of people every waking moment of his life.

As we read the Gospels, we find that in addition to using his mobile miracle clinic for cases requiring physical therapy, fever reduction, and orthopaedic surgery, he also utilised it to heal gynaecological disorders. The Gospels inform us of a woman who had been plagued with an unyielding menstrual flow for twelve years (Matt. 9:20-22; Mark 5:25-34; Luke 8:43-48). Not only was she in a continual state of discomfort, but religious laws deemed her unclean. Formerly a woman of means, she had consulted the best specialists on Harley Street and at the Mayo Clinic, but none of the treatments was effective. After many years of trying, her resources were exhausted and she was forced to come to terms with the reality that although money can pay for cosmetic surgery, it cannot buy health. At the end of her rope, she noticed that Jesus was in her town and broke all the laws of ritual purity as she pushed through the crowds to get close to him. She risked everything, knowing that if she was recognised she might be stoned for breaking the law. This woman didn't want to converse with Jesus, she simply wanted to touch his garments. Luke says the woman approached Jesus from behind while others were pressing against him, and touched his garment — not his body, but his garment! Her faith was so great that she believed that if she could touch something that had touched Jesus she would be healed. Sure enough, Jesus experienced a power surge and asked the strangest question to the pressing crowd, 'Who *touched* me?' The restored woman nervously identified herself, and Jesus rewarded her with the words, 'Daughter, *your* faith has healed you.' The healing was only possible because the woman had faith in Jesus' ability to heal.

The factor of faith in Jesus' ability to heal is also raised in the account of the healing of the two blind men (Matt. 9:27-31). These men are prime examples of the definition of faith found in Hebrews 11:1. They had heard about Jesus' miracles but, being blind, were physically unable to verify any of the cases. Nonetheless, they were determined to be restored. So tenacious were they, that they even followed Jesus into the house where he was staying. Testing their faith, Jesus asked them the all-important question, 'Do you believe that I am able to do this?' It was only after they unwaveringly responded in the affirmative that he touched their eyes and pronounced, 'Let it be done for you according to your faith.'

Another intriguing example of healing faith occurs in the story of the ten men with leprosy (Luke 17:11-19). Adhering to the strictures of ceremonial etiquette, these 'unclean' men stood at the prescribed distance from Jesus and shouted their request for healing. Jesus did not summon them to his presence and grant them instantaneous healing, but instead commanded them to present themselves before the priests. According to Jewish law, only the priests could certify a person cured of leprosy. Although not yet healed, the men responded to Jesus' command. This was indeed a brave act of faith, for had they arrived at the temple in their 'unclean' state they could have been stoned to death. The exemplary nature of their faith is further appreciated by the fact that they would have had to travel a great distance over an extended amount of time to get from the border of Samaria and Galilee to Jerusalem. The text informs us that the men were cleansed while in the process of going to the priests. This is one of the most powerful examples of faith healing in the Gospels and gives hope to the millions of people whose faith is not immediately rewarded with healing. It may take days, weeks, months or even years for faith to become sight, but all who seek healing must be willing to take the journey that leads to the high priest who is able to 'sympathise with our weaknesses' (Heb. 4:15).

In addition to experiencing healing as a result of exercising their own faith, there are several examples in the Gospels of people being healed vicariously through the faith of others. Often, the vicarious healing miracles took place in the context of parent-child relationship. Apparently, mature people are expected to have a measure of faith but children are often innocent and helpless victims of the devil's ploys. When Jairus's daughter got sick to the point of death (Matt. 9:18-19, 23-36; Mark 5:21-24, 35-43; Luke 8:40-42, 49-56), Jesus calmly assured her father, ' "Do not be afraid any longer, only believe." ' Although the crowds laughed at Jesus he was able to speak life into the lifeless corpse. As the account of the deaf and dumb boy at the foot of the Mount of Transfiguration illustrates, Jesus was even willing to perform healing when the parent's faith was not very strong (Matt. 17:14-18; Mark 9:14-27; Luke 9:37-43). By his own admission, the boy's father confessed, 'I believe, help my unbelief.' Jesus was not concerned about the unbelief, he was just glad he had something to work with, and as a result of a parent's faith the young boy was restored to juvenile wholeness. Faith is such a powerful instrument that even pagans who approached Jesus on behalf of their children were rewarded. Among them was the Canaanite woman (Matt. 15:21-28; Mark 7:24:30). At the end of their dialogue Jesus commended the woman, 'Great is your faith, let your wish be accomplished.'

Sin and Sickness

As we rehearse these amazing accounts of miraculous healing, some may be wondering why Jesus did not just go ahead and eradicate all sickness. Wouldn't this have been the compassionate thing to do? Didn't he come to make the world a better place? If we were to ask Jesus, he probably would tell us that this is the very mission he accomplished. As the crucified Messiah he broke the stronghold of every force that oppresses humans. However, the life of faith demands that all who follow Christ must wait until the second coming to experience the full effects of his sacrifice. Although we can't see it, we must believe that he has 'borne all of our infirmities and healed all of our diseases'. Until perfect health becomes part and parcel of our everyday lives, the Christian must face the paradoxical reality of living in a world that is still affected by sin.

Sickness was never a part of God's plan for his creation. When God created the earth and its inhabitants, he pronounced everything good. The whole concept of aging and pain were not even in God's plan. It was only after our primogenitors decided to rebel against God that disease and discomfort invaded our planet. Yahweh warned Eve that she would experience pain in childbirth, and Adam was told to expect strained muscles and limiting fatigue as he toiled in the soil. With the necessity for Adam to sow, till, and reap, there is also a suggestion that if the humans refused to do their part there was a possibility of starvation. When death entered the world, sin also introduced harmful bacteria that polluted the water and affected the longevity of the plant food that formed the basis of the first family's diet. It was also possible for dietary choices and lifestyle habits to affect a person's genetic code, resulting in the transmission of certain diseases to future generations. Because of sin, we have to accept sickness as a natural part of life.

As the story of the man born blind demonstrates (John 9:1-34), sickness does not discriminate among its victims. Sinful habits do not mandate that a person will be sick any more that inner righteousness guarantees a person's physical health. Seeing the man in his pitiful condition as he begged by the roadside, the disciples asked Jesus, 'Rabbi, was it this man's sin or his parents' sin that caused him to be born blind?' The disciples' question had nothing to do with genetics, but was a reflection of the superstitious belief that a person's disability had to be linked to a particular act of sin. They saw it as God's judgement on individuals, much like the pastor in Montgomery who attracted controversial attention when he posted a sign on his church's billboard that read, 'AIDS is God's judgement upon homosexuals'. Jesus knew that the contracting of disease was much more complicated than God arbitrarily picking sinful segments of the world's population to serve as object lessons to the rest of us. He knows that the majority of people who carry the human immunodeficiency virus are heterosexuals and newborn infants. Thus he responded to the disciples, 'Neither this man, nor his parents sinned.'

A person does not have to be a sinner to be affected by sickness. When a child is born with Sickle Cell Disease, he has simply inherited dominant genes that have been passed on by his parents through countless generations. When airborne bacteria, carrying strains of deadly viruses, plague communities and countries, they don't check each person's spiritual status before they attack the immune system. According to the Bible, Job was a man who was perfect in all his ways, yet when Satan assaulted him he was covered with painful abscesses from his head to his toes. Godly men and women have been permanently maimed in accidents caused by moving vehicles, workplace machinery, household hazards, warfare or terrorism. Innocent children are born with undiagnosable diseases. Millions of people are constantly harassed in certain seasons of the year when the weather disturbs mischievous allergens that evoke runny noses, swollen glands, and teary eyes. Sickness is just a part of sinful reality.

However, this is not to say that lifestyle habits cannot affect a person's health and that of those in her immediate circle of influence. The link between lifestyle and sickness is seen in the healing of the man by the pool of Bethesda (John 5:1-18). When Jesus met the man in the temple later on that Sabbath, he advised him, 'Don't practise sin any more, so that nothing worse happens to you.' Again, in the account of the healing of the paralysed man, Jesus pronounced the patient's sins forgiven before proceeding to the healing ceremony (Matt. 9:1-8; Mark 2:2-12; Luke 5:17-26). Many people are sick because of the destructive choices they make in life. Some people are afflicted with certain diseases as a direct result of their lifestyle practices. Sexually-transmitted diseases are *chiefly* contracted by people who are engaged in promiscuous or homosexual behaviour. Lung cancer and urological disorders are usually stimulated by smoking or the consumption of alcohol. Cancers that affect the digestive system, hypertension, cholesterol and obesity are usually related to an unbalanced diet. Some congenital diseases are also the direct result of destructive parental habits like smoking crack, drinking alcohol, or unhealthy nutrition.

Seeing that some sicknesses are avoidable, to a certain degree anyone can participate in Christ's compassionate ministry of healing. It can be done by simply encouraging healthy lifestyles. There are times when it is OK to repeat the saying, 'Physician, heal thyself.' In this microwave age where we have become accustomed to quick results, it's easy for people to expect instant healing so they can be well enough to eat another sodium-drenched, high-cholesterol TV dinner with a clear conscience. However, the first step to holistic well-being is acknowledging that we are primarily responsible for our health choices. It is presumptuous for people to assume that God is obligated to heal them if their lifestyles promote death by prolonged suicide. Jesus' admonition to the healed man from Bethesda is a clear reminder that our choices can impact our health.

Some of the sicknesses that Jesus cured were placed under the catch-all phrase of 'demon possession'. The fact that all sickness is a result of sin, and consequently engineered by Satan, suggests that sickness and disease as a whole are demonic. However, the Gospels indicate that there *are* times when demons choose to inhabit individuals and manifest themselves in diagnosable diseases. In one instance a man was brought to Jesus who was possessed with a demon that rendered him mute (Matt. 9:32-34). The Synoptic Gospels also include a story about a demon-possessed man in the Gadarenes who lived in a cemetery (Matt. 8:28-34; Mark 5:1-20; Luke 8:26-39). Based upon the available data, in which we discover that a legion of demons had established residence in this poor man's body, a modern psychiatrist would probably diagnose him with a multiple personality disorder. Additionally, judging from his symptoms, as well as being deaf and dumb, the young man who was brought to the disciples at the Mount of Transfiguration would probably have been diagnosed with epilepsy (Matt. 17:14-18; Mark 9:17-27; Luke 9:37-42). In all of these instances, healing came only after the demons were expelled from the victims' bodies.

Again, these cases in no way suggest that every sick person is playing host to a demon. You don't need to call the pastor to cast demons out of you the next time you get a migraine. Had it not been for the demonic factor, there is a possibility that each of the cases I have mentioned would have been treatable with modern medicine and therapy. However, having said this, it must never be forgotten that sickness is a constant reminder that Satan still has influence in this world. It is Satan's attempt to cast doubt on the power and promises of God. This is why it is so important that God's people show compassion to the sick and provide them with the hope of everlasting health in the earth made new.

Ultimate Healing

As impressive as exorcisms may seem, as much as they neutralise the devil's authority and let him know who is really in charge, no healing miracle is as offensive to Satan as when a person is divinely selected to defy the grip of death. Death is supposed to be the devil's final victory – the point at which he won in Eden. All the suffering and agony humans experience is merely a torturous prelude to certain death. However, with the assurance of Jesus' victory on the cross, the devil has been issued a notice of eviction and has been relieved of the keys to hell and the grave. Several times during his earthly ministry, Jesus infuriated Satan by temporarily calling individuals back from death's prison house. For a people who anticipated a general resurrection with the advent of Messiah, these miracles provided hope.

One of the first to experience the joy of resurrection was Jairus's daughter (Matt. 9:18-26). When Jairus first approached Jesus and asked for his assistance, his daughter was at the point of death. It was as Jesus ventured to his home that the woman with the issue of blood touched him in faith. Jairus must have found it hard to be patient knowing that his daughter would soon breathe her last. When they finally arrived at the home, the 12-year-old girl was dead and the mourners were already crowding the hallways getting ready for the funeral. Jesus was not despondent or worried. He simply walked into her room and took her lifeless hand. As he touched her, the warmth of the same life-giving Spirit that had breathed into Adam at creation energised the girl and her pale, cold body became irradiated with life.

As impressive as the young girl's resurrection was, the Gospels record another that makes it look simple. This one took place in Nain, a village close to Capernaum (Luke 7:11-17). While walking through the village, Jesus passed the house of an unnamed widow and noticed That a hearse was parked outside. He stopped and watched as the people mourned and the pallbearers carried out the coffin containing the corpse of the widow's son. It had already been embalmed and prepared for burial. The funeral director had already been paid. The insurance company had already sent her a policy cheque to help defray expenses. As Jesus watched the procession and sensed the loss in the widow, who probably depended on her son for assistance and companionship after the loss of her husband, he was moved to compassion. There is no indication that the widow asked Jesus to help, but the scripture informs us that he approached her and asked her not to weep. This must have been a strange request coming from a man she did not even know. No! it was an *impossible* request. How could she stop weeping when her son was about to be placed in a tomb? Before she could respond, Jesus stopped the funeral procession, knocked on the coffin as if he were knocking on the young man's bedroom door, and spoke to him like a father who didn't want the boy to be late for school, 'Young man, I say to you, arise.'

If you think that this resurrection was impressive, wait until you hear about the one performed in Bethany of Judaea (John 11:1-44). This was the *creme de la creme* of all miracles that Jesus performed. While he and his disciples were miles away from Bethany, Jesus received a message from Mary and Martha that their brother Lazarus was sick. By the time Jesus arrived in Bethany, Lazarus had been dead for four days. Unlike the synagogue official's daughter, Lazarus was not in a darkened room. Unlike the widow of Nain's son, Lazarus was not in the coffin on the way to the cemetery. Lazarus had already been *entombed*. His body had already started to deteriorate. Maggots had already started eating away at his skin. His heart had not beat in ninety-six hours, neither had breath passed through his body. But when Jesus stood outside at the face of the tomb and called him by name, somehow his life-giving voice resounded on Lazarus' eardrum causing it to vibrate and start a chain reaction throughout his body. First the brain was stirred into action, and then the heart began to pulsate – first slowly as the thick, coagulated blood changed, gradually thinning to normal. As the blood rushed past each cell, muscles and ligaments were awakened to the point that the fullness of life once again invigorated Lazarus' body. The text tells the story of how Lazarus was energised so efficiently that he came out of the tomb.

Before raising Lazarus, Jesus had to remind the grieving Mary who he was. He wasn't just a miracle worker bringing temporary happiness to broken families, he was 'the resurrection and the life' (John 11:25). He was the one through whom the curse of death would be eternally broken. He was the one who would free all the prisoners in Hades. The people of Judea were given an opportunity to witness Jesus' power on the afternoon he was crucified.

After Jesus had breathed his last, Matthew informs us that tombs were opened and many saints were raised from the dead (Matt. 27:52-53). No names are provided, but it stands to reason that they had been in the tombs a lot longer than Lazarus. As if waiting to greet Jesus, the newly-resurrected saints remained until Sunday morning before exiting the tombs and making surprise appearances in Jerusalem.

As far as we know, Jairus's daughter, the widow's son, Lazarus, and the unnamed saints who were raised on Good Friday eventually returned to the grave. Ultimate resurrection does not take place until the Messiah returns to establish his kingdom of peace. Nonetheless, all of these resurrections point to the surety of God's promises. The future resurrection also gives hope to all who ail as a result of disease, accident or age. Healing is promised to all. It may not come when the elders perform an anointing service. It may not even come if we change lifestyle habits. Some of us will have to see the grave first, but Paul promises that a mystery will take place in the resurrection, 'This destructible body shall become indestructible, and this mortal body shall assume immortality' (1 Cor. 15:53).

Conclusion:
Heal the Sick

We may sit back and marvel at Jesus' healing miracles and reason that he was only able to do what he did because of his supernatural power. However, we must never forget that Jesus performed his miracles as a human being who had fully submitted his will to God. He was being used in ways that had only been witnessed earlier in the ministries of Elijah and Elisha. The manifestation of the Holy Spirit through healing miracles was demonstrated through Jesus' disciples. When he commissioned the twelve apostles, he exhorted them to 'heal the sick, raise the dead, cleanse the lepers, [and] cast out demons' (Matt. 10:8). In fact, he gave similar instructions to the larger group of seventy disciples with the words, 'heal those who are sick, and say to them, "The kingdom of God has come near to you"' (Luke 10:9). The Holy Spirit worked so powerfully in the seventy that they returned announcing, '"Master, even the demons are subject to us in your name"' (Luke 10:17).

The healing power of God was also mightily demonstrated in the early church. Soon after Jesus' ascension, the apostles Peter and John encountered a lame man begging for alms in front of the Beautiful Gate in Jerusalem. Feeling compassion for the man, Peter replied, '"I don't have silver or gold, but that which I do have I will give to you. In the name of the Lord Jesus Christ, take up your bed and walk!"' (Acts 3:1-11). The man immediately responded in faith and went away leaping, shouting and praising God. News of the healing soon spread throughout the city, and soon many sick people sought out the apostles for healing. In fact, so mightily was the Holy Spirit working through the life of Peter that people were healed just by allowing his shadow to move over them (Acts 5:12-16). Peter was so filled with the Holy Spirit that he was even able to perform the ultimate in healing — resurrection. When he visited Joppa and discovered that Tabitha had died (Acts 9:36-43), he went to her place of abode, where she had already been prepared for burial, and simply spoke the words, 'Tabitha, wake up!'

Although it appears that all the apostles were involved in healing, Luke mentions only the miracles conducted by Peter and Paul. While in Lystra with Barnabas, Paul encountered a man who had been crippled from birth (Acts 14:8-12). Moved by compassion, Paul commanded the man to stand on his feet. As the man responded in faith, he was able to experience full use of his legs for the first time in his life. So impressive was the Spirit's working through Paul, particularly in Ephesus, that Luke reports, 'God did extraordinary miracles through Paul, so that when the handkerchiefs or aprons that had touched his skin were brought to the sick, their diseases left them, and the evil spirits came out of them' (Acts 19:11-12). As with Peter, Paul was also used by the Spirit to perform the ultimate healing miracle. During a late-night service in Troas, a young man named Eutychus fell asleep and fell three storeys out of a window (Acts 20:1-12). Needless to say, he died – probably from a broken neck. When Paul touched him, life once again blessed his mortal body.

These are wonderful stories, but we must never think that healing miracles cannot be a part of *our* reality. The same God who worked through Elijah and Peter is willing and able to work through twenty-first-century disciples. Although there are many counterfeit healers who claim to be working under God's power, we cannot deny the Spirit's ability to reward the faith of the afflicted with restorative blessings from above. In Mark's account of Jesus' farewell speech to his disciples, we read the promise, ' "These signs will accompany those who have believed: in my name they will cast out demons, they will speak with new tongues; they will pick up serpents, and if they drink any deadly poison, it shall not hurt them; they will lay hands on the sick and they will recover" ' (Mark 16:17).

The same wonder-working power that was endowed on these disciples of Jesus is available to the people of God today. We may not all be blessed with the gift of calling people to instantaneous wholeness, but we can all play a part in alleviating sickness and disease in our society. Jesus himself healed in different ways. Sometimes he did just declare a person whole. However, there were times when he had to lay his compassionate hand on them and let them feel the special touch of love. On other occasions, the person being healed had to do something practical. As you engage in the ministry of healing, consult the Spirit to determine the method for which you have been equipped. Maybe the Spirit has gifted you with the rare ability to speak people to wholeness through prayer. Your method may be the gift of touching people through the medical arts, or just plain old tender loving care. Or God may have gifted you with the skill of helping people perform practical acts of lifestyle reform. Whatever the method of healing with which the Spirit has gifted us, we can all work to make a difference in society as, together with the compassionate Christ, we provide people with an opportunity to experience a taste of the kingdom in this world of sin.

Reflect

1. Since the ultimate resurrection does not take place until the second coming, what was the purpose of Jesus' raising people from the dead if they had to die again?

2. How is it possible to tell whether a professed faith-healer is working for Christ or Satan?

3. Do medical doctors possess the gift of healing?

4. Why do some people get healed after an anointing service while others continue in pain and end up dying?

5. Jesus had three major methods of healing: (a) spoken word, (b) laying on of hands, (c) practical act. Browse through the gospels and categorise all his miracles under these three headings.

Apply

1. Form a prayer band with the express purpose of praying for sick people once a week. Record all results in a prayer journal.
2. Evaluate your personal health habits and assess whether you need to 'heal yourself'. Plan a six-month agenda for better health.
3. Learn a sign language and practise sharing short inspiring stories to young deaf children.
4. Encourage the health leader in your church to sponsor easy-to-run health programmes that will be of interest to the community (e.g. healthy cooking, aerobics classes, conflict resolution, stop smoking).

Chapter 5
Blessed are the persecuted

*' "Be blessed when people despise you
and persecute you and charge you
with every evil falsely on my account.
Be happy and express praise,
because your reward is great in heaven" '*
Matthew 5:11-12.

Among the controversial themes evoked by *The Passion of the Christ* is the issue of religious persecution.

The story of Christ's suffering is one that reflects the will of the powerful majority over the disenfranchised minority.

On one level, loyal Jews were being persecuted by the Romans who saw it as their duty to maintain social order and engender loyalty to the state. On another level, there was religious persecution within Judaism as certain influential sects sought to protect their own agendas. Jesus was a victim of both Roman and Jewish religious persecution. Although a Jew himself, his radical teachings and calls for systemic reform had caused him to be ostracised by the religious establishment. The religious authorities were also concerned about the popular following he had garnered and felt that if he continued to gain support Rome would be forced to come down heavily on the entire nation. In fact, Rome's compliance with the trial and crucifixion was spurred on by the charge that Jesus claimed to be the messianic king poised to overthrow Caesar.

Long before his betrayal and arrest, Jesus knew that his persecution was inevitable. His brave actions against the religious establishment had biased minds against him from early in his ministry when he had chased the business people from the temple. John's gospel paints him as a fugitive against whom the authorities had issued an arrest warrant. They had just been waiting for the opportunity to bring him down. As far as the leaders were concerned, Jesus had to be stopped because he was a threat. In fact, this is the root cause of all religious persecution. Governments or ecclesiastical powers usually allow for some deviance in the social order, but once an influential voice rises that threatens the cohesion of the *status quo* they revert to persecution. Persecution is only necessary when authorities deal with people of conviction. Had Jesus been a person who was simply seeking coverage on the evening news, he would have silenced himself at the first indication that he had upset the powers that be. No. He had a clearly defined purpose, refusing to allow threats to deter his plan of action.

Jesus warned his followers that persecution was not unique to his own experience, but would also come to them. For practically all of their time with him, the disciples had been able to minister unhindered. However, in his sermon on the Mount of Olives, Jesus issued a warning to them and all Christians in consequent ages: '"They will hand you over for persecution and they will kill you, and you shall be persecuted by all nations because of my name"' (Matt. 24:9). It was not too long after the ascension of Christ that his followers were being persecuted by the same Jewish authorities and their counterparts in various cities in the Roman world. After a while, persecution became part and parcel of Christian witnessing. So common was persecution to the Christian minister that Paul cautioned his young protégé, Timothy, ' "All those who are living godly in Christ, will be persecuted" ' (2 Tim. 3:12).

Over the two millennia of Christianity, faithful Christians in different parts of the world have been continuously persecuted. In the first century, persecution came primarily from the leading Pharisees and Saducees. After a while, when Christianity began to attract a number of non-Jews with its message of a new king and kingdom, the Roman government took over from the dispossessed Jewish leaders and continued persecuting Christians for the next three centuries. When Christianity finally took hold in the Roman Empire and became more politicised, persecution of faithful Christians was carried out at the hands of the established Catholic and Orthodox churches seeking to preserve the often pagan traditions that had become part and parcel of majority Christianity. Even after the Protestant Reformation, persecution of the faithful came at the hands of some of the 'reformed' churches. At this very moment, faithful Christians around the globe are being persecuted by oppressive 'Christian' governments. These sufferers are joined by countless others in atheistic and non-Christian countries who choose to serve God even though they know they face imprisonment or even death. It is to these victims, and to others who will join them, that the compassionate Christ offers words of comfort as he encourages them to be happy in their suffering. For the rest of this chapter, we will attempt to come to terms with the rationale behind Jesus' strange admonition to the persecuted.

Military Strategy

In a previous chapter, I mentioned that some Jewish opponents of *The Passion of the Christ* charge that the movie has the potential for stirring up a new wave of antisemitism. Judging from some major events in Christian history, this is not a groundless fear. Protestants, Orthodox, and Catholics alike have persecuted the Jews. Who can forget the mindless Jewish massacres encouraged by German Reformer Martin Luther and his political heirs? Even the pejoratively termed Falasha Hebrews of Ethiopia have experienced political persecution under the hands of their Orthodox Christian siblings. However, there is another reason why some Jewish critics would rather the story not be told. While few dare to raise the issue, the more piercing matter for modern Jews is the portrayal of Jesus as the Jewish Messiah. When the story of the crufixion is told, many twenty-first-century Jews probably feel as crushed and embarrassed as the first-century Jewish leaders who witnessed the Roman soldiers attaching the inscription to the top of the cross: 'Jesus of Nazareth, King of the Jews.'

Jesus did not fit the expected profile of the Messiah – not even for his disciples. Not many think about the fact that Jesus' warm reception when he rode into Jerusalem on Palm Sunday was punctuated by the crowd shouting ' "Hosanna!" ' Modern hymns often use 'hosanna' as a term of adoration, but in reality it is a battle cry: 'Deliver us now!' The people recognised Jesus as Messiah and were asking him to do what a liberator was supposed to do. The Jews had a rich history of resilience and could point to warrior Messianic figures like Moses, Joshua, David, and Judas Maccabees. If this carpenter's son were the *real* Messiah, then surely he too would resort to violent methods of overthrowing the imperial oppressors. But Jesus of Nazareth was different. He had not sought an alliance with the Zealots, a Jewish 'terrorist' organisation that was intent on expelling Rome from the occupied territories in Palestine. And he didn't seem in the least bit responsive to the crowd's chants for deliverance.

BLESSED ARE THE PERSECUTED

Instead, Jesus would further embarrass the nation by enduring the humility of arrest and abuse without so much as a protest. How could this persecuted sage be the Messiah of the people? How could the helpless, bruised and mangled body on that Roman instrument of torture be the eternal king of the nations? Hadn't he claimed to be the anointed one when he gave his inaugural sermon in the synagogue at Nazareth? Hadn't he promised to break the yoke of oppression? Hadn't he guaranteed to usher in the year of Jubilee? Wasn't he the one who had awakened the consciousness of the huddled masses and offered them a glimmer of redemptive hope? If he were God's Anointed, why would he allow himself to endure such suffering?

These were all fair questions, but had the crowds been listening to Jesus' teachings they would have known that Jesus had come with a different agenda. While the nation was focused on the temporal grip of imperial Rome, there was a bigger threat from powerful universal spiritual forces that did not manifest themselves in flesh and blood. The problem of oppression was not just a Jewish issue, but one that affected the entire inhabited world. As impregnable as they seemed, even the Romans were under siege. Although it may not have appeared to be the case, Jesus did come to earth to serve as commander of a liberation army. However, his recruitment efforts would not focus only on a righteous militia from the Jewish faithful, but would also include warriors from 'every nation, tribe, language and ethnicity.'

Since the enemy was spiritual, the international Messianic resistance movement had to be trained in the art of non-conventional spiritual warfare. The years Jesus spent on earth were dedicated to establishing military strategy more radical than Sun Tzu or Mahatma Gandhi. It was a strategy that was governed by the same compassion that exuded from his persona as he walked the dusty roads of Palestine bringing light to dark places and joy to heavy hearts. Jesus' strategy did not model itself after the proven techniques of Tirhaka, Nebuchadnezzar, Darius, Alexander the Great, Pompey or Julius Caesar. He did not even consult the military chronicles preserved in the books of Maccabees, or arrange for a conference with the leaders of the Jewish Essenes, who lived in the desert of Qumran and had written several documents on how to prevail against the Roman enemy. Instead, when Jesus opened his mouth to teach his recruits, he told them they could only win this important war if they loved their enemies. He instructed them to turn the other cheek when struck by an attacker. He exhorted them to offer the mugger the emergency money they had hidden in their shoes.

With his radical pacifist teaching, Jesus negated the very factor that legitimised the people's hope for a successful revolution—the *lex talionis*. Translated 'law of retaliation', *lex talionis* is a Latin term theologians use to describe the law that was at the heart of Israelite civil code. This was the law that demanded an eye for an eye, a tooth for a tooth, a hand for a hand, and a life for a life. With his insistence on non-violent resistance, Jesus made his followers very vulnerable. In an age when honour demanded revenge, they were being asked to swallow pride and let their assailants walk away. This refusal to respond would be taken as weakness and would eventually open the door to persecution. However, Jesus did not ask his followers to assume a posture that he himself was not willing to take. As a result of his conviction, Jesus would also be persecuted to the point of death.

Citizens of an Alien Kingdom
Many Christians throughout the ages have embraced Jesus'

non-violent message as a foundational Christian doctrine. The historical accounts of the early church in the New Testament are in stark contrast to the bloody history of God's people that stain the pages of the Old Testament. Although they were growing in large numbers, the early Christians did not view themselves as an earthly political entity which needed to protect territory or people with brute force. When their fellow Christians were arrested, imprisoned, stoned, exiled, beheaded or crucified, the first weapon they turned to was prayer. This method of warfare proved successful, and by the fourth century the insignificant minority from Palestine had grown into a majority religious force in every corner of the Roman Empire. That the non-violent emphasis remained a mainstay of Christianity is suggested in the historical theory that attributes the demise of the Roman Empire to the acceptance of Christianity by Roman soldiers who refused to kill the enemy. More recently, the non-violent example of the compassionate Christ was also instrumental in the success of the movements against the apartheid systems that kept Blacks oppressed in the United States of America and South Africa.

Jesus' advocation of non-violence is a part of his overall message concerning the ethical demands of people who wish to be a part of his kingdom. Some modern theologians have adapted Jesus' ethical teachings to New Age theories, and propose that it was Jesus' intention to encourage people to establish the kingdom in their own strength. They suggest that his vision was similar to Gandhi's doctrine of *satyagraha*, which teaches that people's combined 'soul force' can ultimately transform oppressive governments. While the peaceful resistance movements headed by Mahatma Gandhi, Martin Luther King and Nelson Mandela ultimately led to governmental transformation, they were not able to stamp out the evil spirits that kept the politically liberated communities under bondage. It is for this very reason that the message of Jesus was not intended to create earthly communities of peace, but to transform individuals for the eternal kingdom of peace that had been inaugurated but not yet made manifest.

Christians are forced to live their lives in an uncomfortable paradox. They are citizens of an eternal kingdom that is destined to supersede every earthly kingdom. However, in the sphere of earthly reality, this kingdom has no recognisable borders, no economic system, and no visible state house. Citizens of this kingdom are truly called to walk by faith and not by sight. The fact that the kingdom has not yet taken a physical form does not give the citizens an excuse to live as if they were citizens of this age. Hence, Jesus enjoins all who are called by his name to live as if they are already in that kingdom. In fact, Paul identifies the Christian as the one who does not focus 'on things that are seen, but on things that are not seen; for the things seen are temporary, but the things not seen are eternal' (2 Cor. 4:18).

As citizens of an alien kingdom, the choices Christians make in this life will often conflict with the demands of earthly governments. When a person commits fully to the peaceful path of Christ, he may have to say 'no' to government efforts to draft him into the military in times of war; she may have to show kindness to her avowed enemy; he may relinquish the right to divorce his wife after she has broken the sacred vows of marriage and had an affair with another man; she may even refuse to pledge allegiance to idolatrous symbols of national pride. These are not easy decisions to make for people who are attached to earthly communities with defined guidelines for social interaction and orchestrated pressure to show loyalty to the state. The one who is faithful to God might be forced to make decisions deemed unpatriotic or nonsensical. Knowing the societal backlash that is inevitable when people decide to live for God, Jesus alerted his disciples with the words: ' "Do you think that I have come to give peace on earth? No, I tell you, but rather division; from this time households will be divided. . . father against son and son against father, mother against daughter and daughter against mother, mother-in-law against her daughter-in-law and daughter-in-law against her mother-in-law" (Luke 12:51-53). Jesus realised that decisions for the kingdom would come at a great price. He knew that households and communities would be affected beyond repair. He understood the inevitability of chaos and disorder as the ideology of the kingdom clashed with the norms of the world.

The ideological divide between kingdom dwellers and their worldly neighbours is illustrated in a number of parables in which Jesus compares the two groups, the weed and the wheat, sheep and goats, and good fish and bad fish. Conflict will always be a part of earthly reality because all the citizens of the earth are either aligned to Christ or Satan. Many wishing for an earthly utopia joined Rodney King, who tried to stop the rioting and violence in Los Angeles by appealing to people's sensitivities. As this victim of police brutality faced an international audience through the power of media, he pleaded to the infuriated mob and their racist provokers, 'Can't we all just get along?' In response to his question, Jesus would have answered, 'No, we can't all get along!' Or as Bob Marley put it in his musical adaptation of the speech that Haile Selassie presented before the League of Nations when opposing the spread of Italian fascism: 'Until the philosophy that deems one race superior and another inferior is finally and permanently discredited and abandoned; until the basic human rights are equally guaranteed to all without regards to race; until there are no more first and second class citizens of any nation; the dream of lasting peace and world citizenship will remain but a fleeting illusion to be pursued but never attained.'

It would be nice for all the world to get along, but as long as evil forces continue to possess the hearts and minds of humans the desire for unity amounts to wishful fantasy. And as long as spiritual powers influence people to revel in sin, Christians will always be an unwelcome nagging voice in society. When Christian leaders campaign for godly family structures headed by a husband and wife, the liberal media dismisses them as old-fashioned bigots who are intolerant of alternative lifestyles. When concerned Christian parents protest against the demoralising programmes being fed to their children in state schools and on the airwaves, they are accused of being against free speech and mixing church concerns with affairs of the state. When conscientious Christian politicians and preachers decry pre-emptive military strikes on defenceless nations, they are maligned as unpatriotic traitors. The very fact that there will always be moral tension between Christians and worldly society means that Christians will always be potential victims of persecution.

Character Building

The message of Christianity is one that provokes the earthly agents of Satan and places God's people on the path of persecution. Because of this, it is necessary for Christians always to be prepared for the inevitable. Preparation for persecution takes place at the very moment a person says 'yes' to the Gospel. Jesus was very honest in his teaching about the journey to the kingdom. The final destination is a glorious paradise with untold joys. However, the path the Christian must travel in the meantime is not always attractive. There are pleasant stretches on the winding and hilly trail, but if a traveller remains on it long enough he will face trials and tribulations. When Jesus commissioned the twelve disciples (Matt. 10:16-30), he let them know that they would be like 'sheep in the midst of wolves' who would be arrested, flogged and betrayed. Like lifelong soldiers, after each experience they are expected to jump into the battle again.

The unattractiveness of the path is also illustrated throughout the Sermon on the Mount. In the Beatitudes, the first section of the sermon (Matt. 5:3-11), the citizens of the kingdom are described as being spiritually poor, mourners, meek, and persecuted. This is a profile of a people who have no reason to be happy on earth. They have been affected by death, poverty, powerlessness and persecution. Further, in the section dubbed the Antitheses (Matt. 5:21-28), Christians are instructed to endure abuse when attacked, and demonstrate love to their enemies. With these and other hard sayings, it is no wonder that towards the end of the Imperatives — the final section of the Sermon (Matt. 6:1-7:29) — Jesus informs his disciples, ' "The gate is narrow and the way is difficult that leads to life and there are only a few that find it" ' (Matt. 7:14).

For those who consider giving up, Jesus puts things into perspective. If he, as the Master, had to undergo ridicule and persecution, then surely those who follow him must be prepared to endure the same. Unfortunately, too many professed Christians are unwilling to face the fury. As early as the second century AD, Christian writers like Justin Martyr tried to make Christianity more palatable to the pagan mind by merging its symbols with the cult of Mithra. By the time the Roman empire embraced Christianity, there was hardly any difference between the church and the state. Nowadays in professed Christian nations, church leaders have no problem selling their souls to the state. Very few have the courage to direct prophetic injunctions to unjust governments, and many churches place the nation's flag in a prominent position in the sanctuary – as if it deserves a place next to God as an object of worship. Governments may be able to restrict physically and socially, but they have no authority over the spiritual.

Jesus emboldens his followers to stand firm to divine principles even when threatened with the death penalty: ' "Don't fear those who can kill the body but have no power to kill the soul; rather fear the one who has the power to cast both body and soul into hell" ' (Matt. 10:28). Some may read this as a threat to those who are thinking about leaving Christianity, but it is really a word of encouragement. A Christian may cave in to political pressure to avoid capital punishment, but in the day of judgement she will be punished for turning her back on God. As called-out people, we emulate Joseph who chose imprisonment over adultery. As ambassadors of God, we follow Moses and Esther, who placed the welfare of their people over political accolades. We may choose to enjoy the pleasures of sin for a season and miss out on eternal pleasure in the afterlife; or forsake earthly pleasure now and enjoy an eternity of unparalleled and indescribable ecstasy. Paul puts the Christian experience in perspective when he suggests that all the negative assaults a Christian endures can be compared to a single blink in the eyes of eternity (2 Cor. 4:16-18).

Since persecution is an ever present threat on the Christian path, it behoves the traveller to face it with a positive attitude. Paul considered trials as a spiritual obstacle course that helped make him stronger for the kingdom. In his triumphant ode in Romans he defiantly dismisses the demons of hardship, distress, persecution, famine, nakedness, peril and the sword as feeble attempts to separate the

Christian from the love of God (Rom. 8:35-39). He recognises that these are merely instruments of Satan, who would like the child of God to cry out, ' "My God, my God why have you forsaken me?" ' But even when Christians feel alone, it is the memory of the very Jesus who uttered those words on the cross that assures them of God's everlasting love. It is the assurance of the One who promised, ' "I will never leave you or forsake you," ' that gives them the strength to fight another day.

In his attempt to express the essence of the Christian journey, the late James Cleveland penned a one-verse gospel song: 'I don't feel no ways tired, I've come too far from where I've started from, nobody told me the road would be easy, I don't believe he brought me this far to leave me.' Many share Cleveland's testimony as they face the trials of each day with more tenacity than they faced those of the day before. However, there are others who are still on the path but admit to being tired. Their muscles are enfeebled and it does not seem as if they can take another step. It takes all the energy they can muster to make it over a mountain; only to discover that there is a treacherous incline that demands superhuman strength to surmount. It is probably the experience of the tired folk on the journey that inspired someone to modify the words of Cleveland's song from 'I don't feel no ways tired', to 'I just can't give up now.' The apostle Paul expressed it another way, 'We have this treasure in clay jars, to show that the superlative power belongs to God and not to us; we are always under pressure but not crushed; perplexed but not despaired; persecuted but not deserted; thrown to the ground but not destroyed; always bearing the death of Jesus in the body, so that the life of Jesus may be manifest in the body' (2 Cor. 4:7-10).

Vengeance is Mine

By this time, you are quite possibly wondering why a chapter like this is placed in a book on the compassion of the Christ. So far we have described a Christ who encourages his followers to face danger with extreme tenacity. How does this demonstrate compassion? For some it may sound cruel for an all powerful potentate to watch as the ones he claims to love are exposed to pain and suffering. Why doesn't he just put an end to everything before other innocent lives of Christian soldiers in the line of duty are snatched away? Better still, why doesn't he endow faithful Christians with supernatural powers that can outperform the best in modern weaponry?

These were some of the very thoughts that plagued the mind of John the Baptist as he sat on death row in Herod's fortress. He had devoted his entire life to the ministry of the Messiah. He had never participated with the children in his community when they performed pranks on unsuspecting neighbours. He had resisted the temptation to experiment with alcohol, tobacco and illicit drugs in his youth. He never knew what it was to dance all night in a club. He had never even been romantically involved with a woman. While his classmates were building their businesses and starting their families, he was living in a cave by the Jordan River. While other men his age sought amusement at the Roman theatres and market places, he was preaching to anyone who would listen. Like Christ, his message was relentless and uncompromising as he called everyone to accountability – religious leaders, government workers, common people, and even Roman soldiers.

John must have thought all his sacrifices were worth it when Jesus finally appeared at the Jordan one day. His preaching had not been in vain – the Messiah of prophecy had come into the world. He did not even feel bad when

Jesus' ministry became more popular than his own. Before Jesus came on the scene, people would travel for miles to come and hear John. However, Jesus went to the people, and his message – though the same – was presented in a more joyful tone than John's. When John's disciples complained about the success of Jesus' ministry, John humbly replied, 'I must decrease, so that he can increase.' As far as John was concerned, all his years of faithful service would soon be rewarded when his cousin, the Messiah, declared himself king and established the kingdom of peace. John was probably not even ruffled when he was arrested and placed in prison. He may have even told his cell-mates that he was not concerned about the trumped-up charges against him because his cousin was soon going to break down the doors of the jailhouse and pronounce him free.

After a while, John's hope turned to dismay. He had been waiting for Jesus to manifest himself as Messiah, but every day when he consulted the newspaper Jesus was featured in a different light. He probably would not have minded if the media depicted an outlawed Jesus eluding the authorities after inciting crowds to overthrow the government. However, Jesus' face kept appearing in the society section as gossip columnists described him as a celebrity who attended glitzy parties in the evenings, and entertained his growing audiences during the days. The despondent John began to doubt. Did he sacrifice his childhood for nothing? Was this Jesus a fraud? Would people view *him* as a fraud for preaching the imminent judgement and proclaiming that Jesus was the one through whom this judgement would come?

In a desperate bid to relieve his confusion, John sent a message to Jesus through some of his disciples, ' "Are you the one who is to come, or should we be expecting another?" ' (Matt. 11:3). Many Christians who go through persecution ask the same question. They know that God wants everyone to repent, but what about the welfare of those who have already repented? They know that salvation comes to the one who endures to the end, but how long will it be before the end? Jesus did not provide John's messengers with a detailed explanation for his suffering, he simply invited them to follow him around for a day. As they witnessed the ministry of Jesus first-hand, they saw the blind receive their sight, the lame walk. Leposy was cleansed, the deaf heard, the dead were resurrected and poor people responded positively to the liberating Gospel of the kingdom (Matt. 11:5-6). The Bible does not say how John received the news from the messengers, but he must have been forced to a rethink. The Messiah was not merely an agent of divine wrath, but was a channel of divine love. He was so compassionate in his desire to see every soul in the kingdom, that he was willing to give them a taste of the kingdom on this side of eternity. John had to come to terms with the strange reality that even his current persecution was a direct result of the Messiah's compassionate plan to seek and save the lost.

Hopefully, John also understood that Jesus' ministry of unprejudiced compassion did not obliterate the inevitability of the messianic judgement. The Messiah who suffered for the sins of humanity is very much aware of the pain experienced by those who are persecuted for righteousness' sake, and will not let their tormentors go unpunished. He takes a record of every tear and each drop of blood that has been shed; he personally examines every bruise that has been inflicted; he carefully stores every limb and body part that has been severed. He controls himself from responding too quickly to the souls under the altar crying, 'O holy and true Lord, when will you start judging and avenging our blood on those who inhabit the earth?' (Rev. 6:10).

In spite of his teaching about peace and love, Jesus in no way negated the necessity of a final *Armageddon*. He did not shatter the emancipative expectations of the rebel Zealots, the reclusive Essenes and the oppressed masses; he simply put them on hold. In fact, even while involved in his ministry of compassion, Jesus expressed his disappointment that the cataclysmic reversal had been postponed: ' "I came to cast fire upon the earth; and would that it were already kindled." ' (Luke 12:49). The compassionate Christ knows that evil must be eradicated and the unrepentant persecutors of God's people must be avenged, but he requests that the saints exercise patience in suffering as they await the culmination of God's ultimate plan.

As God's people seek justice for their suffering, they can be assured that the divine court is preparing to prosecute the persecutors. The impartial God who knows the motives of every heart has taken the right to avenge from the hands of fallible humans and has entrusted to himself the work of vengeance. 'Vengeance is *mine*, says the Lord! I will repay!' (Rom. 12:19). Paul reminds the sufferers in Thessalonica, 'It is the right thing for God to afflict those who are afflicting you and to bring relief to all who are being afflicted, when the Lord Jesus is revealed from heaven with his powerful angels in flaming fire, inflicting vengeance on those who do not know God and who did not obey the gospel of our Lord Jesus' (2 Thess. 1:6-8). All who have been victims of crime can take comfort in knowing that there will be an ultimate administration of the *lex talionis* (law of retaliation), in which God himself will be the executor. Those who suffer can find comfort in knowing that although 'weeping may endure for a night, joy comes in the morning' (Ps. 30:5). The compassionate Christ will reward them for their patience.

Conclusion:
God is Love

Many people find the concept of an avenging God problematical. They don't understand how a God of love can shower plague and pestilence on sinners. However, God's act of judgement is simply a part of his overall plan to expel sin and its influences from the universe. Those who are victims of his wrath have consciously chosen their destiny through their decisions in life. He who was 'wounded for our transgressions, and bruised for our iniquity' (Isa. 53:5) has already borne the sins of humanity. Nobody has to perish and face God's retributive justice unless they express a desire through their constant rejection of the Holy Spirit and the sacrifice of Christ. In rejecting Christ, they reject salvation and choose damnation. It would be an uncompassionate God who forced people to live in a kingdom they despised. In a strange way God's judgement on sinners is an act of compassion.

It was belief in the righteous judgement of God that gave hope to the African slaves in the Americas. In the midst of their hardships and persecutions, as they encountered famine and sword, they would look through the eyes of faith over the Jordan River and see 'chariots coming for to carry [them] home'. It was with the hope that they would 'Ride on the Chariot in the Morning, Lord', that they sang, 'I'm so glad that trouble don't last always.' And don't think that they didn't know about the ethic of the kingdom, for whenever they were tempted to rebel and render evil for evil, they would sing, 'I would not be a murderer, I'll tell you the reason why, for if my Lord would come and find me, I wouldn't be ready to die.' At times, they even preached to their masters who beat them on Saturday night and went to church on Sunday morning: 'Everybody talking 'bout heaven ain't going there.' They knew that one day, Michael would stand with the heavenly hosts, and the cry would go out: ' "Let the evildoer still do evil, let the filthy still be filthy, let the righteous still do right, and the holy still be holy. Behold I am coming soon, bringing my recompense, to repay every one for what he has done" ' (Rev. 22:11-12).

This promise is good news for the Christians who are being physically persecuted today in Sudan, Saudi Arabia, China, Greece, Nigeria, Indonesia, Malaysia, Pakistan, Poland, Russia, France, Egypt, and a number of other countries around the globe. While they fight the good fight of faith as exiles in a strange land, they accept persecution as an occupational hazard and await the avenging God who has promised to deliver. Until then, they sing with the legendary Thomas A. Dorsey, 'Precious Lord, take my hand, Lead me on, let me stand, I am tired, I am weak, I am worn; Thru' the storm, thru' the night, Lead me on to the light, Take my hand, precious Lord, lead me home.'

Reflect

1. Why does God allow his people to go through persecution?
2. What does it mean to be 'persecuted for the sake of righteousness'? Is persecution an indicator that a person is living a godly life?
3. How does this discussion relate to non-Christians who are victims of religious persecution?
4. What is your reaction to the suggestion that the vengeance of God is a demonstration of his compassion?

Apply

1. Search the Internet or your local library for information on countries where Christians are currently being persecuted. Make a list of the countries and pray for your fellow believers on a regular basis.
2. Send a care package to a missionary family serving in a dangerous area of the world. Be sure to include a note of encouragement.
3. Seek out a person who is the only Christian in his or her family and invite them to fellowship in your home at least once a month.
4. Continually assess your physical and spiritual health to prepare yourself for persecution.

Chapter 6
We have an Advocate

*'My little children,
I am writing these things to you that you may not sin,
however if a person makes a mistake and sins,
we have an advocate with the Father, Jesus Christ
the righteous; and he is the atoning sacrifice for our sins,
not just for Christians but for the entire world.'*
1 John 2:1-2.

Most people who have viewed *The Passion of the Christ* leave the cinema with feelings of sadness, solemnity and guilt. Ironically, some of the same people testify that it was the most powerful portrayal of the Gospel they have ever witnessed. While the testimonies are probably sincere, it is extremely troubling that people would mistake the movie for 'the Gospel'.

The word 'gospel' is from the Old English and literally means 'good news'. It is the good news about the arrival of the Messiah who has initiated the establishment of the eternal Kingdom of God.

It is the good news that Christ has triumphed over the evil powers of death, hell, and the grave. It is the good news that the faithful will one day live in a world from which sickness, dying, pain and all other evils are absent.

It is true that there are several components to the gospel *story*, and the passion of Christ is an essential part. However, Christ's passion means nothing apart from the incarnation, submission, crucifixion, resurrection, ascension, intercession and exaltation. When the gospel story is told correctly, people should not be left with a condemning cloud of doom, but with a redeeming rainbow of hope.

Those who have not been exposed to other aspects of the gospel will leave *The Passion of the Christ* with the erroneous impression that Jesus' story started in the garden of Gethsemane where he uttered his agonising prayer, and ended in the garden near Golgotha where he was entombed.

However, the Bible provides a more comprehensive picture of a story that starts with the advent of sin in the garden of Eden, and ends with the restoration of the saints in the garden of the New Jerusalem that surrounds the tree of life.

Unlike the movie, the Bible does not leave us with an empty feeling of guilt and helplessness. It does not leave us trying to guess what happens next. The Bible is clear that every episode in the life and ministry of Jesus serves as a prelude to the wonderful climax when evil is destroyed and righteousness reigns forever. The passion, crucifixion and resurrection are all important, but as we await the final revelation of his glory, twenty-first-century Christians ought to be concerned about what Jesus is currently doing in the scheme of salvation.

What *is* Jesus doing now? Some sincere Christians believe that he is waiting for 144,000 people to overcome every iota of sin in their lives and live as perfectly as he did. When this is accomplished, they purport, his Father will be vindicated and he will be given permission to usher in the kingdom. Other Christians believe that he is present on earth in an invisible form establishing the foundations for a

New World where faithful witnesses will be charged with the conversion of every unrepentant human who ever lived. Certain liberal Christian groups believe that his remains still reside in an unmarked tomb in Palestine and the only place he really exists is in the memories of his followers. While these theories can engender lively discussion, the Bible is very clear what Jesus is doing now. During his farewell speech to his disciples at the last supper, Jesus shared his ascension plans with them. ' "Don't allow your hearts to be disturbed," ' he exhorted, ' "Since you believe in God, you can also believe in me. . . . I am going to get a place ready for you, and when I am finished I will come again so that we may be reunited and be able to live in the same place." ' (John 14:1-3). At this very moment, Jesus is preparing a place for his followers in his Father's kingdom.

Present in His Absence

On a human level, when we think about Jesus' preparing a place in his Father's mansion, it's not hard to imagine him personally inspecting the plans for the accommodation reserved for the redeemed saints. With information from the one who knows the very number of hairs on the body of each creature, he could be making sure that ever detail conforms to our individual taste. He could even be ensuring that the landscaping includes our favourite trees and flowers and the pantry is packed with our preferred foods and beverages. Indeed, the prophet Isaiah when speaking of the messianic age did say, 'They shall build houses, and live in them; and they shall plant vineyards and eat the fruit of them. They will not build houses for others to live in, or plant food for others to eat.' (Isa. 65:21-22). In the place that Jesus is preparing, there will be no oppressive class system in which peasants slave to build the wealth of the aristocracy. Each person will be on equal status in the Father's kingdom.

It's all well and good that Jesus is preparing a place for the redeemed, but why is it taking so long? When he spoke to his disciples, he gave the distinct impression that he was coming soon. In one instance he prophesied that some will not see death before he returned in his glory. All the New Testament writers attest to his soon coming, but it has been almost two thousand years and he is nowhere to be seen. Has he forgotten about us? We've come to the point in Christian history where some denominations have stopped believing in the second coming and are asking the question of the scoffers, 'Where is the promise of his coming? For ever since the fathers died, things have remained as they were from the beginning of creation' (2 Peter 3:4). In their embarrassment over the delay, other Christian denominations have embraced New Age theories and advocate building the kingdom of God through our own efforts.

Although the delay has been long, a quick review of biblical history lets us know that God works in his own time. Indeed, Peter echoed the Psalmist's recognition that 'one day with the Lord is as a thousand years and a thousand years is as a day' (2 Peter 3:8). When Jesus said he was coming soon, he meant it, but he also knew that he had to rely on his Father's clock. By his own admission, with his limited knowledge, he did not know the exact date and time of his coming. This information, he declared, was only known by the Father. This is the same Father who threatened to wipe out humanity with a flood, and then waited four hundred years to execute his plan. This is the same God who gave a promise of Messiah to Adam and Eve in the garden, and waited four thousand years before implanting Jesus' incarnated embryo into the womb of Mary. God works in his own wisdom, and in his own time, and the coming kingdom is as sure today as it was when it was first announced by the Hebrew prophets.

While Jesus waits for his Father to announce the time of the end, he is not idly passing time sky boarding to different planets with juvenile angels. He is actively working for the salvation of humans. It should bring a sense of consolation to his followers to know that in at least two of the occasions where Jesus is visioned in heaven, he appears to be actively involved in the affairs of humans. When Stephen was being stoned to death, he was blessed with a vision of heaven where he saw 'the Son of Man standing by the right hand of God' (Acts 7:55-56). Jesus was not sitting comfortably like a spectator enjoying a gladiator show, he was standing in protest. John also gives the impression that Jesus is actively moving around heaven working in behalf of our salvation when he speaks of the Lamb approaching the throne of God and receiving the scroll of salvation that only he could open (Rev. 5:6-7). While it might seem as if Jesus has forgotten us, he is very much involved in our daily affairs.

In fact, although Jesus is limited to the courts of heaven *physically*, he has never really left us alone *spiritually*. He may be absent from this earth, but he is always present. When he delivered his farewell speech to his disciples on the night he was betrayed, he informed them that it was to their advantage that he went away (John 16:7). While on earth, he could be at only one place at any given time, but through the agency of the Holy Spirit he could be present everywhere. Before he ascended into the heavens, he assured his disciples with the words, ' "I am with you every day, until the completion of this age" ' (Matt. 28:20). Although we can't see Jesus in person, his presence is assured. The popular gospel hymn, 'In the Garden', by C. Austin Miles reminds us of Jesus' continuous presence: 'He walks with me and he talks with me, and he tells me I am his own, and the joy we share as we tarry there, none other has ever known.'

Legal Intercession

Even as Jesus communes with us through the presence of the Holy Spirit, he is primarily engaged in the work of intercession. This again helps to explain why it has taken so long for him to return. Peter assures us, 'The Lord is not negligent in his promise as some consider negligence, but is patient to [us], because he does not wish for a single soul to be destroyed but for all to partake in repentance' (2 Peter 3:9). At this very moment, Jesus is pleading the case of sinners before the Father, hoping that every person on the face of this earth has a chance to experience redemption.

From the perspective of divine law, every person on this earth deserves eternal damnation. The Bible is clear that 'the wages of sin is death' (Rom. 6:23), and 'all of us have sinned' (Rom. 3:23). The scriptures define sin as 'lawlessness' (1 John 3:4). Some would like to limit the definition of sin to the transgression of the Ten Commandment law, but it is much more than that. Sin is personified in the spirit of rebellion that coerces people blatantly to disregard laws that promote harmony in the social and divine orders. As Jesus illustrated in the Sermon on the Mount, there may be many people who outwardly keep the Ten Commandments but are inwardly rotten to the core. Sin is not manifested merely in bad actions, it is ingrained in bad persons. It is as much a sin to slander a person as it is to commit mass murder. It is as much a sin to overeat as it is to take an overdose. It is as much a sin to watch pornography as it is to engage in extramarital sex. Sin is so serious, that even the right thing done with the wrong motive may be abhorrent to God (Rom. 14:23).

It is precisely because sin is so dangerous that John makes a special plea in his letter to Christians, 'My little children, I am writing these things to you so that you may not sin, but if anyone does sin, we have an advocate with the

Father, Jesus Christ the righteous' (I John 2:1). When John makes this appeal, he is fully aware of the deep-rooted nature of sin in the Christian. He had already declared, 'If we say that we have no sin, we deceive ourselves, and the truth is not in us' (1 John 1:8). None can claim perfection. The most pious individuals in your church are carrying sin around with them. While this revelation may be taken by some as an excuse to revel in iniquity, it must be quickly pointed out that John is simply echoing the fact that we are born in sin and shaped in iniquity (Ps. 51:5). He is not promoting the erroneous view that the Christian is helpless when it comes to living a righteous life. In fact, the text states the exact opposite. Immediately following his declaration about the sinfulness of humans, he provides a word of hope: 'When we confess our sins, he who is faithful and just will forgive us our sins and cleanse us from all unrighteousness' (1 John 1:9).

The fact that God is 'faithful and just' does not give Christians an excuse to sin. However, the mere fact that we 'have sin' means that it is *possible* for us to sin. Paul addresses the Christian's struggle in Romans with his discourse on the war between the 'law of God' and 'the law of the flesh' (Rom. 7:13-25). The Christian knows the right thing to do, but sometimes he ends up doing the wrong thing. It's not that he plans to do it, but sometimes when his spiritual guard is down the flesh creeps in and claims a brief victory. Understanding the pressure of living a godly life in a sinful world, God, in his compassionate mercy, has provided a system of appeal in which the guilty can be acquitted. A mistake in a person's life does not have to be a death sentence. A temporary error does not have to be equated to a fatal bullet that rips through the sinner's heart. The 'faithful and righteous God' is willing to evaluate each case before the final verdict is rendered.

The Christian can find comfort in knowing that she does not have to face the Almighty God by herself, for she has 'an advocate' with the Father. The word advocate is derived from the Latin *advocatus* which is a translation of the Greek *parakletos*, meaning 'one called to be beside'. In Roman society, the advocate was the attorney who represented his client in court. In no uncertain terms, John depicts Jesus as the sinner's defence attorney. Jesus is not one of those high-priced attorneys who argue precedent-setting cases before the Supreme Court or at the Old Bailey, he is a court-appointed public defender who offers his services to anyone in need. Even those who have the monetary resources opt for Jesus to represent them because he has the most impressive record in legal history: he has never lost a case.

Jesus is one of those attorneys who is constantly criticised for putting guilty people back on the streets. None of the people who come to him is innocent of the crime. They all deserve to die. The victims of their crime will all agree that they deserve the death penalty. However, the compassionate Jesus is always able to convince the court to dismiss the charges. Unlike shrewd lawyers who spell their profession with the letters l-i-a-r-s, Jesus does not have to resort to deception and twisting the facts to secure the acquittal of his clients. When he approaches the Judge, his Father, he tells him the truth. He acknowledges that his defendant has broken the royal law. He admits that the defendant is worthy of death, and then he puts forth his argument. It is the same every time. 'Father,' he says, 'You said that if this person confesses her sins, your faithfulness and righteousness will compel you to forgive her and restore her to sinless perfection.' He then proceeds to explain that the Holy Spirit has informed him that the sinner is genuinely repentant for her transgression and has made a commitment to walk the path of righteousness.

The Spirit is also referred to as an advocate in John's gospel. This is not immediately clear since most Bible versions translate the Greek *paracletos* as 'comforter' or 'counsellor'. The legal role of the Holy Spirit is clearly seen in his role of convicting the world about 'sin, righteousness, and judgement' (16:8-11). Whereas Jesus works as the defence attorney, the Holy Spirit works as the prosecuting attorney. Although the court should be a place of justice, it is the usual practice in most courts of law for attorneys to win their case at any cost. Prosecutors and defenders attack each other with vigour, and are more concerned with adding a victory to their record than the innocence or guilt of the defendant. But justice reigns supreme in the heavenly court. Judge, prosecutor and public defendant work together for the defendant. While God the Father listens to the appeal of the Son of God, the Spirit of God 'searches the individual's heart' (Rom. 8:27). Although the prosecutor, the Spirit automatically knows when a person is sincerely repentant and encourages the defence attorney to make his case to the Judge.

With all the court in favour of acquittal, the sinner needs not fear. God himself opened the way for sinners to approach him with their crimes, 'Come, let us discuss your problem together,' he says, 'If your sins are currently like scarlet, I promise you I will make them as white as snow; if they are currently like crimson, I will make them as wool' (Isa. 1:18). And Hebrews gives the assurance that we will not be alone: 'Having a great high priest who has entered heaven, Jesus the Son of God, let us remain true to our confession. For we do not have a priest who is unable to sympathise with our weaknesses, but was himself tempted like we, yet he does not have sin. For this reason, let us approach the throne of grace with confidence, that we may receive mercy and find grace to assist us at the right time' (Heb. 4:14-16).

Ceremonial Intercession

The reference to Jesus as a high priest elevates the ceremonial aspect of Jesus' intercession. Ceremonies are occasions in which an important event is either instituted, celebrated or commemorated. Usually in a ceremony, there is an established procedure that dictates the role of each participant and the basic elements that are needed in order for the ritual to have meaning. For example, unless centuries-old tradition is broken, the next monarch of England must be part of a coronation ceremony at Westminster Abbey which is presided over by the Archbishop of Canterbury and is sealed with the placing of an authentic jewel-studded crown on the sovereign's head. Similarly, the President of the United States is always sworn in by the Chief Justice of the Supreme Court and must affirm an oath while placing his hand on the Bible (Billy Graham's prayer is optional!). The ceremonies involved in Jesus' intercession commemorate the forgiveness of sin, and the reconciliation of forgiven humans to a righteous God.

Although Jesus did not actually assume his role as intercessor until a specific point in history, the ceremonies commemorating his intercessory activity were instituted with the advent of sin. After creating Adam, Yahweh warned him that the penalty for disobedience was death. However, when Adam and Eve did disobey, they did not immediately die – in fact, he continued living for hundreds of years. We discover later, that the reason why Adam did not see immediate death was due to God's merciful provision that the life of a clean animal would be used as a vicarious substitution for human life. In recapping the story of Abel's sacrifice, the book of Hebrews informs us that after sacrificing an animal with the right spirit, the sinner was declared righteous (Heb. 11:4). The efficacy of animal sacrifice as a substitution for sin-induced human death is also demonstrated in Yahweh's instruction to Noah after the flood (Gen. 9:5). The recognition that animal life was intended to atone for human sin is evidenced in the fact that practically all the religions of antiquity demanded animal sacrifice to appease the 'gods'.

Probably in a bid to distinguish his genuine system from the pagan counterfeits, the Lord decided to establish an official ceremony of grace with the Israelites. This was not just to be an occasional ceremony, but one that continued throughout the year. The plan he shared with Moses revealed an elaborate system that demanded the investment of large amounts of funds and hundreds of dedicated workers (Exod. 25:1-28:43). The actual place in which the ceremony was to take place would be constructed from the highest grade material and exquisitely adorned with the most expensive metals and stones. Even the main priests who administered the rites were to be dressed in ornamental garments that rivalled the Crown Jewels in the Tower of London. When Israel had built its sanctuary – and the temples that came later – everybody knew that this was a special place for a special purpose. One could not help but marvel at the palatial beauty that signified the merciful plan of the Sovereign God.

Upon entering this magnificent wonder of the ancient world, the worshipper would at once be struck with feelings of awe and solemnity. At the centre of the hall framed with towering gold laden pillars and hand woven curtains, was a gigantic altar. This altar seemed out of place in the midst of such elegance. Upon the altar lay the carcases of clean animals which were being slowly roasted by a controlled fire. Attention to the altar was also garnered by the bloody rituals being administered by the priests. At any time during the day, you could witness them thrusting razor sharp knives into the jugular veins of bleating sheep and braying goats, and wringing the necks of cooing doves and squawking pigeons. Then they would take the draining blood from these recently slaughtered animals and sprinkle them on the altar. Once the blood had fully drained, the animal was offered to God.

The priests who officiated in the sanctuary were not just putting on a show for tourists. They were fulfilling their role as intercessors between sinful humans and a holy God. Every animal they sacrificed represented a human being who had sinned and come to the temple to make things right with the Creator. As the confessing sinner looked into the animal's eye while the knife was plunged into its innocent neck, he was to see his own reflection and emotionally experience the pain of death. It was to be such a horrifying reminder of the wages of sin that he would determine in his mind to walk the straight and narrow path. In a gesture commemorating the sinner's cleansing, the priest would eat a portion of the burnt offering, symbolising the complete transferal of the individual's sin to a divinely appointed human representative.

As impressive as the sanctuary ceremonies were, they were only a symbol of a divine reality. No element in the system had the inherent ability to wipe away human sin. Everything pointed to God's ultimate plan in which his beloved Son would permanently restore the broken relationship between humanity and divinity. More than any biblical book, Hebrews meticulously displays how the Israelite ceremonial system finds its fulfilment in the intercessory ministry of the compassionate Christ. Throughout the book, the Messiah is portrayed as the embodiment of the entire sacrificial system – the one who gave meaning to the rituals.

In reading Hebrews, we quickly learn that every animal sacrifice and priestly worker finds complete fulfilment in Christ. One passage summarises it beautifully:

'But when Christ came as a high priest of the good things

to come, then through the greater and perfect tabernacle (not made with hands, that is not of this creation), he entered once for all into the Holy Place, not with the blood of goats and calves, but with his own blood thus obtaining eternal redemption. For if the blood of goats and bulls, with the sprinkling of the ashes of a heifer sanctifies those who have been defiled so that their flesh is purified, how much more will the blood of Christ, who through the eternal Spirit offered himself without blemish to God, purify our conscience from dead works to worship the living God!' (Heb. 9:11-14).

Here we clearly see that Jesus intercedes for us, both as priest and sacrifice. As priest, he represents his people to God – he has been appointed and anointed to render an acceptable sacrifice. As sacrifice he represents the repentant sinner – he is the one who absorbs our sins and receives the death which should have been ours.

The old ceremonial system was cumbersome, costly, discriminating, and inconvenient. It was laden with human limitations and tainted with ungodly corruption. This is not to say that it did not serve a divine purpose – it had been initiated by God himself. However, it was never meant to be the *means* through which sins were ultimately forgiven, it merely served as an object lesson for God's real method of restoring humanity to his image. In the place of the blood of animals, Jesus has offered his own blood to the Father. This is not just any type of blood, it is the life-giving blood of the one through whom life was originally given to humanity. It is not the blood of Joseph or Mary, it is the powerful blood of God himself. This is the perfect blood that flowed through the veins of Adam before sin. It is not Type A, B, or O qualified by rhesus negative or positive terminology, but it is Type S for Salvation. It is this perfect blood, uncorrupted by sinful human DNA, that Jesus offers his Father in behalf of humanity. This is the blood that was deposited in the heavenly haematology laboratory and is available to every repentant sinner who desires to be transfused with eternal life.

The efficacy of Jesus' offering is illustrated by John's description of him as 'the atoning sacrifice for our sins, not just Christian sins, but the sins of the world' (1 John 2:2). The Greek term translated here as 'atoning sacrifice' is rendered in some Bible versions as 'propitiation' and in others as 'expiation'. The term 'propitiation' conjures the image of an exacting god who can only be appeased with an offering that meets his specifications. The offering only becomes acceptable after he has examined it and chosen to accept it. Only then will he pardon the sinner. On the other hand, 'expiation' refers to an offering that the divinity is obligated to accept, simply because it has been offered. The sinner does not have to wait for confirmation from the divinity, but knows that he is forgiven at the very moment the sacrifice is made.

Jesus' sacrifice has elements of both. The expiatory power of the sacrifice is seen in the fact that Jesus was the perfect offering that God demanded, and as such God was obligated to forgive the world. Even those who have never heard the name of Jesus were forgiven by his offering. Hence, Paul would say 'God was in Christ, reconciling the world to himself' (2 Cor. 5:19). However, as a result of human fallibility, Christ's sacrifice also has a propitiatory aspect. God has accepted his sacrifice, but he remains in his priestly role before the divine throne, continuously interceding for the repeated sins of struggling saints. It is with this assurance that Hebrews exhorts, 'Since we have the confidence to enter the Most Holy Place by the blood of Jesus (a confidence made possible when he opened a new and living way for us through the curtain, which is really his flesh), and since we have a great high priest over the house of God, let us approach with a true heart in full confidence of faith, our hearts having been sprinkled from an evil conscience and our bodies washed with pure water' (Heb. 10:19-22).

Conclusion:
Nobody's Fault but Mine

Although Jesus is no longer physically present on earth, it is comforting to know that he is still involved in his ministry of compassion. He is not oblivious to the struggle that the Christian experiences in his attempt to live a holy life in this world of sin. In fact, at the very moment when we face temptation he offers his assistance through the voice and power of the Holy Spirit. The same compassionate Christ who invites us to share in his holiness reminds us that we 'have not experienced any temptation that is not a part of human experience; but the faithful God will not allow anything to come our way that we can't handle, but always provides a way of escape' (1 Cor. 10:13). Even in the face of temptation, we must never believe that he has left us alone.

Knowing the nature of sin, Christ also understands why some Christians submit to temptation and neglect to capitalise on his succouring presence. While it is possible for Christians to thwart *every* attack from the devil through the power of the Spirit, Christ knows that former habits and environmental factors contribute to a person's ability to resist temptation. He is very aware that some people have not learned to vision victory in the face of apparent defeat. And so with his tender compassion, he responds to their cries for help and rescues them from the grip of the enemy, providing them with new strength to face another day. He continues to beckon struggling Christians to the higher path of righteousness, and offers the solution for victory: 'Would you be free from the burden of sin? There is power in the blood, power in the blood! Would you o'er evil a victory win? There is wonderful power in the blood!' His perfect blood has the wonder working power to plant our feet on the higher ground of righteousness.

With the knowledge that Jesus is faithfully contending to secure the salvation of each individual, the Christian can face the future with confidence. While we dare not presume on the grace of God and hold on to cherished sins with the erroneous impression that a loving God will never discipline us, we have the assurance of knowing that 'If we confess our sins, God who is faithful and righteous will forgive us, and cleanse us from all unrighteousness.' We can praise God in knowing that Jesus has secured the means by which every person who desires can receive salvation. Indeed, it is this confidence that inspired the words of the old Negro spiritual, 'It's nobody's fault but mine, nobody's fault but mine, if I die and my soul is lost; it's nobody's fault but mine.'

Reflect

1. How do we know that Jesus is present with Christian believers through the agency the Holy Spirit? Does he commune with non-Christians?
2. Since we have all inherited sin, is it possible to live a life of victory over sin?
3. The Israelites had an elaborate ceremonial system to remind them continuously of God's plan of salvation. What system do modern-day Christians have?
4. Is there ever a time when Jesus stops interceding for a sinner?

Apply

1. Conduct an analysis of your Christian experience by comparing the issues with which you struggle now, and the issues you faced when first accepting Christ. How has your progress been? What are you going to do about it?

2. Try your hand at calligraphy and write some texts about God's love for humanity on large index cards. Mail them as postcards to ten people who have not yet accepted Christ as their personal Saviour.

3. Invite some friends to assist you in writing a four-person play based on the court room scene in heaven. The characters should be the Father (judge), Son (defence attorney), Holy Spirit (prosecutor) and the sinner. Arrange for the play to be rehearsed by competent actors and presented in a public venue for non-Christians.

4. Ask your church secretary for contact information on non-attending members. Give them a call or send them an e-mail or card, and let them know that you are thinking about them. Be sure not to engage in a discussion over why they stopped coming to church – just show that you care!

Conclusion

*'What does the Lord require of you?
To do justice, to love mercy,
and to walk humbly with your God'*
Micah 6:8.

Although a seasoned Academy Award winning actor, Mel Gibson decided not to take a leading role in *The Passion of the Christ*. However, he did place himself in a minor role. In the film, it was Gibson's hand that held the hammer used to drive the nails through the hands and feet of Jesus as he was secured to the cruel cross. He later explained to interviewers that he felt compelled to do that scene since it was his sins that had placed Jesus on the cross.

Indeed, the truth is that all of us held that hammer and drove those nails through the body of our innocent Saviour; all of us mocked him as he hung with his body shamefully exposed to barbarous voyeurs; all of us gave him vinegar to drink when he asked for water; all of us took hold of that spear that was thrust in his side.

All of us are implicated in Jesus' death.

The question now is, what are we going to do about it?

We can never make amends to Jesus.

It is impossible for us to turn back the hands of time and halt the savage crucifixion.

We are unable to manipulate our genetic dispositions or control the sanctity of our environments.

What has been done is forever sealed in the annals of eternity. With our sinful choices, we have killed Christ and there is nothing we can do to reverse our murderous act.

Fully knowing that we were the real perpetrators, we actively participated in the execution of an innocent man knowing that it was we who should have received the punishment. So what can we do about it?

While we cannot erase our culpability in the crucifixion, we can acknowledge the part we played and repent from the actions that drove Jesus to the cross.

As this book has demonstrated, it is not enough to think about what Christ suffered; we must emulate his works of compassion to ensure that his suffering was not in vain. The sole purpose of Christ's mission was to manifest the love of God to a dying world, and we are called to reflect that love by turning from our sins and embracing the righteousness of God. We are called to pick up another hammer, not the heavy wooden mallet used to torture the Saviour, but the gavel of justice used by the Almighty to pronounce liberty to the world.

The prophet Micah loudly declares the requirements of God in response to his mercy: 'What does the Lord require of you? To do justice, to love mercy, and to walk humbly with your God' (Mic. 6:8).

If we really want to ensure that the Christ did not suffer and die in vain, we must do what the Lord requires. We must champion the rights or the poor, the downtrodden and the oppressed. We must behave as magnetic agents of love to people of all faiths and ideologies. We must model the spirit of grace in our interactions with sinners. We must maintain our redeeming witness in the face of persecution. We must be the healing hands to an ailing world. We must tell the story of the compassionate Christ who ever lives to make intercession for his people.

Maranatha!

NOTES

NOTES

NOTES